RINGS

RINGS

RACHEL CHURCH

V&A Publishing

First published by V&A Publishing, 2011
Victoria and Albert Museum
South Kensington
London SW7 2RL
www.vandabooks.com

Distributed in North America by Harry N. Abrams, Inc., New York
© The Board of Trustees of the Victoria and Albert Museum, 2011

The moral right of the author(s) has been asserted.

Hardback Edition
ISBN 978 1 85177 650 4

Library of Congress Control Number 2011923016

10 9 8 7 6 5 4 3 2 1
2015 2014 2013 2012 2011

Front jacket: Model wearing a ring made by Giulio Veronesi. Italy, c.1960.
Back jacket: Enamelled gold ring, see plate 110.
Page 2: Publicity photograph for *Everywoman* by John French. England, 1965.
Page 5: 'The Big Crime Ring (Size 13 ½)', see plate 154.
Page 12: *The Duke Receiving Precious Stones* by an unknown artist,
from *Le Livre de la Propriété des Choses* by Barthelemy l'Anglais. France, c.1405.
Page 28: *Sir Henry Lee* by Anthonis van Dashorst Mor. Netherlands, 1568.
Page 56: *Madame de Senonnes* by Jean Auguste Dominique Ingres. France, 1814–16.
Page 76: *A Young Woman, Probably Florence Emily, Lady Hesketh,* by Frederick Sandys.
UK, c.1880. V&A: E.1391-1924
Page 92: Poster by an unknown artist, advertising Hart Schaffner and Marx Fine
Clothes, c.1920–29.
Page 106: Model Twiggy shows off her rings in New York, early 1970s.

Designer: Charlotte Heal
Copy-editor: Laura Lappin
Index: Christine Shuttleworth

V&A Photography by V&A Photographic Studio

Printed in Hong Kong

V&A Publishing

Supporting the world's leading
museum of art and design,
the Victoria and Albert
Museum, London

CONTENTS

INTRODUCTION

RINGS ARE THE most common and perhaps the most evocative pieces of jewellery. Worn as a sign of love or as a fashion accessory, to mark weddings, remember the dead, or show religious faith, they hold a multitude of meanings. They might also display less private sentiments, reflecting the currents of politics and public events. This book is an introduction to rings made in Europe and in the Western tradition from the Middle Ages to the present, selected from over 2,000 examples held in the exceptional collection of the Victoria and Albert Museum (V&A), London.

Throughout history rings have followed trends in the wider decorative arts: to study rings is to study a miniature history of art and design, and the influence of many key artistic developments. Designs were disseminated through books, trade in gemstones and jewellery, and itinerant goldsmiths transmitting new fashions. The finished piece of work often resulted, as it does today, from close collaboration between the jeweller and the customer. Rings were traditionally made from precious metals such as gold and silver, alongside the cheaper alternatives of bronze, iron or tin; however, gemstones, enamels, ivory, wood and, for modern jewellers, plastics, acrylics and recycled materials have all found their place.

Although the simplest ring consists of a plain, undecorated hoop, many rings can be divided into three main elements, each of which may receive its own decorative treatment. The hoop, which encircles the finger, can be plain, enamelled, engraved or bear an inscription. The bezel is the most salient part of many rings and might be set with a gemstone, a seal, or an engraved or enamelled design. Some rings have sculptural shoulders to join the hoop to the bezel.

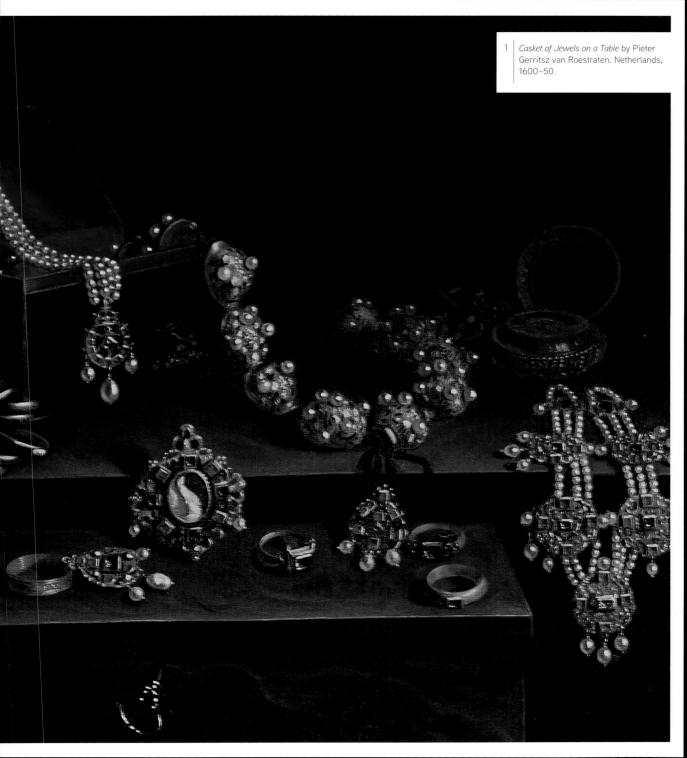

2 | The Townshend Collection on display in the V&A's William and Judith Bollinger Jewellery Gallery.

Maker to Product

ground glass is laid on to the metal surface.

49

The Townshend Gems

Jewellers have used coloured gemstones since antiquity, favouring the natural crystals since around shapes. Later polished as beads or cabochon shaped stones, gems were often faceted to bring out their colour and brilliance, though some stones such in opals are usually colourless become their structure makes faceting difficult.

The exceptional collection of gemstones, set in gold rings, was bequeathed to the V&A in 1869 by the avid collector the Reverend Chauncy Hare Townshend. May were acquired from the Hope collection, home of the famous Hope Diamond, now in the Smithsonian Institute, Washington, DC.

The display shows many of the gem varieties used in jewellery, with the stones grouped according to their natural species. Stones in their natural crystal form can be seen in the Natural History Museum.

Although we have a sense of how rings were worn and owned in the past through portraits, wills and other documents, their makers often remain unknown. Unlike larger pieces of silver, which generally had a maker or sponsor's mark as well as one indicating the purity of the metal, jewellery made before the nineteenth century was not commonly marked. In England the 1738 Plate Offences Act excepted all 'Jeweller's Work' from hallmarking apart from mourning rings. The requirement to mark was extended to wedding rings in 1855, although some jewellers might have voluntarily sent work to be marked before then. John Leigh, a London jeweller who successfully defended himself from an accusation of coin clipping in 1761, set out the rules on metalworking as he understood them:

> As to jewellers' work, there is no act of parliament, nor no rule for a standard, for men to work by, except wedding rings and mourning rings, such we are under an obligation to work standard gold; but for other fancy rings, it is left to the option of the workman: there is no law that binds him to any standard.[1]

Without the constraints of the hallmarking system, the anonymous goldsmiths and jewellers who made rings have tended to be lost to the past. By the eighteenth century, more stringent hallmarking in Europe brought the identity of the maker into view, although many rings relied on contributions from designer, goldsmith, stone-setter and enameller. The great jewellery firms of the nineteenth and twentieth centuries had their own large workshops, but also relied on the assistance of outworkers and small firms. Working in a parallel tradition to the jewellery houses, the individual artist-jewellers of the late twentieth century became presences in their own right.

THE ORIGINS OF THE V&A COLLECTION

THE V&A'S COLLECTION of rings owes its richness to many collectors and donors. One of the earliest influences on the Museum's ring collection was Edmund Waterton (1830–87), son of the naturalist and taxidermist Charles Waterton. Conscious of the standards expected of 'a person of my background and reputation', Edmund rejected his father's eccentric and ascetic lifestyle in favour of every sort of fashionable entertainment. He bought rings 'compulsively and entirely reckless of cost',[2] recording the histories of these rings in his unpublished 'Dactyliotheca Watertoniana'.[3] After what contemporaries described as a 'brief career of pride and folly and extravagance', he ran into debt and was compelled to sell his family home and pawn his collection of more than 600 rings.[4] When he was unable to redeem the pledge, it was offered to what was then called the South Kensington Museum and now forms the nucleus of the V&A's ring collection.

The rings bequeathed by the Reverend Chauncey Hare Townshend (1798–1868), collected as interesting gems rather than as wearable rings, show the range of gemstones used in jewellery. Townshend's collection was later augmented and published by the gemmologist A.H. Church. Aside from his interest in jewels, Townshend was an enthusiastic spiritualist and a friend of Charles Dickens, who dedicated *Great Expectations* to him. This group of 145 rings is of particular interest as it was formed before many of the techniques for artificially improving the colour and appearance of gemstones became widespread. A number of Townshend's rings, including the eight principal diamond rings, came from the collection of Henry Philip Hope (1774–1839), who owned the celebrated Hope Diamond now in the Smithsonian Institute, Washington, DC.

Dame Joan Evans (1893–1977) was a pre-eminent donor to both the ring and jewellery collections. A renowned historian, antiquarian and jewellery collector, she was given by her half-brother, the archaeologist Sir Arthur Evans, the rings collected by their father, Sir John Evans, in gratitude for compiling the index of Sir Arthur's history of the Palace of Minos in Crete. The collection included a particularly rich group of medieval and posy rings. She added to it and completed a series of generous lifetime donations in 1975, graciously thanking the V&A Metalwork Department which 'has been kind to me for 65 years'.

The representation of twentieth-century rings owes much to the generosity of Patricia V. Goldstein (1930–2002), whose lifetime of collecting and dealing in jewellery was crowned by the gift of her collection shortly before her death to the American Friends of the V&A. The archive of the London firm of Godman and Rabey, generously donated by Alan Rabey (b.1932), shows us the workings of a Bond Street jewellery firm and its relationship with major jewellery houses, including Chaumet and Boucheron (pls 3 and 137).

The Royal College of Arts Visiting Artists programme, pioneered by Professor David Watkins from 1987 to 2006, allowed many notable international artist-jewellers to work with students at the college in London. Each created a jewel during their visit and the acquisition of the resulting collection by the V&A has transformed its holdings of contemporary rings.

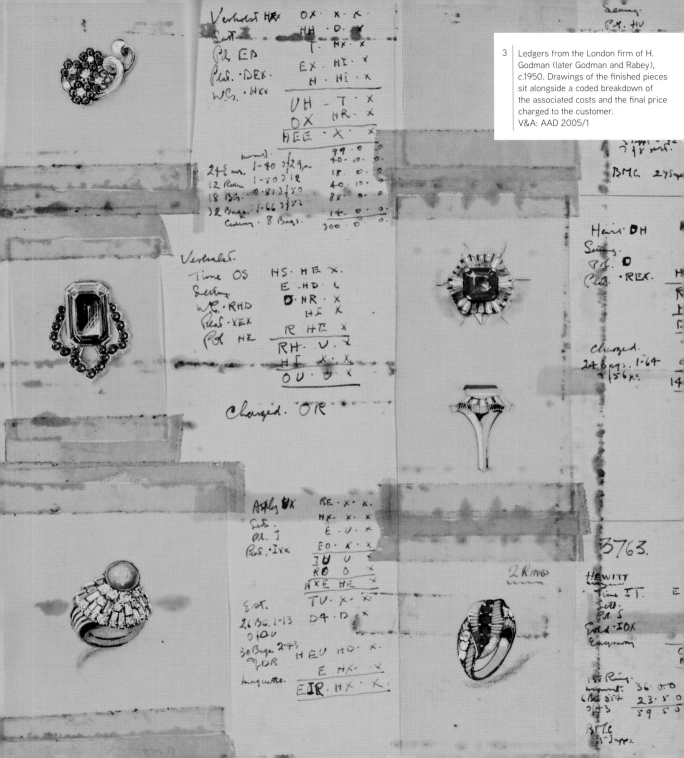

3 Ledgers from the London firm of H. Godman (later Godman and Rabey), *c.*1950. Drawings of the finished pieces sit alongside a coded breakdown of the associated costs and the final price charged to the customer.
V&A: AAD 2005/1

1200 – 1500

JEWELLERY WAS MORE than simply decoration to the medieval wearer. In an age when magic, science and religion were intertwined, a ring could be worn as a sign of faith, as an amulet or to cure illness. The gift of a ring could, as now, signify love or cement social relations. The thirteenth-century English prelate Bogo de Clare purchased 24 gold rings, probably plain rings – one dozen costing 2s and the other 2s 4d – to be given as thanks for small services.[1] The New Year was a traditional time for gifts both personal and official, which were carefully chosen according to the status of the recipient, to affirm allegiances and to promote loyalty. Rings made ideal gifts for these purposes and were often engraved with New Year's greetings on their hoops.

In the early Middle Ages, lapidaries – texts on the properties of gemstones by ancient authors such as Theophrastus and Pliny – were rediscovered and translated. Works such as the *Liber Lapidum* by Marbodus, bishop of Rennes (*c*.1035–1123), attributed magical, religious and symbolic powers to various gemstones. Sapphires were often used on episcopal rings, required to be of gold set with an uncut stone, which were given to bishops at their consecration. They were favoured for their colour, a celestial blue, described by the writer Bartholemeus Anglicus (d.1272) as 'most like heaven in fair weather'.[2] Sapphire rings have been discovered in the tombs of several English bishops, including one allegedly found in the grave of William Wytlesey, Archbishop of Canterbury, who died in 1374 (pl.4).

Rings might be worn in great number for fashionable effect. Portraits from the period show them on every finger, including the thumb and even the upper joints: in a portrait of Lady Joan Beaufort (*c*.1379–1440), she is shown praying with her daughters, each of whom wears a large number of rings; Lady Joan has five on her right hand alone (pl.6). Elsewhere rings are also shown worn on strings around the neck, tied to the wrist, pinned to clothes or attached to hats.

4

Gold ring of Archbishop William Wytlesey, formerly enamelled, set with a pierced sapphire in a claw setting. England, *c*.1350–70. Inside of hoop inscribed 'Willms Wytlesey'.
V&A: M.191–1975

5

Gold ring set with a cabochon sapphire in a claw setting. Europe, *c*.1250–1300. Inscribed 'Amor vincit omnia' ('Love conquers all'), a common inscription taken from Virgil's *Eclogues*, and 'Ave Maria Gra[cia]' (an abbreviation of 'Hail Mary, full of Grace').
V&A: M.181–1975

6 | *Lady Joan Beaufort and her Daughters* by an unknown artist, from the Neville Hours. Paris, *c.*1430–40.

7

8

Between 1150 and 1400 rings set with sapphires, rubies, garnets and spinels became fashionable. Unfaceted gemstones with polished surfaces, known as cabochons, exploited the natural shape of the stone. Around 1400 the point-cut diamond was developed, using the natural pyramidal structure of the crystal. On a ring from this period, the shape of the bezel echoes that of the diamond, tricking the eye into seeing a much larger stone (pl.10).

The gift of a ring to a lover is a custom known since antiquity. The courtly writer Marie de France wrote in the twelfth century: 'If you love him ... send him a girdle, a ribbon or a ring, for this will please him. If he receives it gladly ... then you will be sure of his love'. Andreas Capellanus, writing around 1230 in *The Art of Courtly Love*, felt that

> a woman who loves may freely accept from her lover the following: a handkerchief ... a ring, a compact, a picture, a wash basin, little dishes, trays, a flag as a souvenir, and to speak in general terms, a woman may accept from her lover any little gift which may be useful for the care of the person or pleasing to look at or which may call the lover to mind, if it is clear in accepting the gift she is free from all avarice.[3]

7 | Gold ring (four views). England, c.1300. Inscribed 'Wel were him yat wiste to whom he might triste'. V&A: M.184–1975

8 | Gold ring (three views). Europe, 1400–1500. Inscribed 'Autre ne veuil' ('Desire no other'). V&A: 7125–1860

9 | Gold ring set with a cabochon sapphire. Europe, c.1200–1300. Decorated with chased leaves and dragon heads, its 'stirrup' shape is characteristic of the 13th century. V&A: M.183–1975

10 | Gold ring set with a diamond. Europe, c.1400. Shoulders inscribed 'Ave Maria'. Half of an octahedral crystal has been set as a natural diamond point, polished but not facetted. V&A: M.188–1975

11 | Gold ring set with a cabochon sapphire. England or France, c.1200–1300. The setting allows the sapphire to stand away from the hoop and catch the light. The flaws in the surface have been polished but it remains pockmarked. V&A: 645–1871

9

10

11

12

Diamond rings were often exchanged at weddings or betrothals, combining the strength and unbreakable quality of the stone with the symbolic never-ending circle of the ring. A priest's manual, written by Guillaume Durand in the thirteenth century, describes the diamond as 'unbreakable and love unquenchable and stronger than death, so it suits [the diamond ring] to be worn on the ring finger, the vein of which comes directly from the heart', an idea taken from Roman authors (see p.39).[4]

Romantic inscriptions known as posies, often written in French or Latin, the languages spoken by educated people across Europe, decorate many medieval rings. Whilst some posies were obviously common phrases, others have a more personal feel. The motif of two hands clasped in love, known as a 'fede' from the Italian 'mani in fede' (inspired by the Roman device of 'dextrarum iunctio', or 'clasped right hands'), appears regularly on medieval jewellery (pl.12). It was a sign of loyalty and commonly associated with betrothals.

12 | Silver ring (two views). Possibly Italy, 1400–1500. On one side is a 'fede' of two clasped hands; on the other, two hands clasp a heart. V&A: 848-1871

13 | Gold ring (three views). Possibly France, 1500–30. Outside of hoop inscribed 'Ung temps viandra' ('A time will come'); the inside 'Mon desir me vaille' ('My longing keeps me awake'). V&A: M.221-1962

13

Rings with religious designs or engravings of saints were often worn in the Middle Ages. Individuals might choose a ring bearing an image of the saint whose name they shared, or call upon the belief that each saint could protect against a particular mischance. Appealing to saints was believed to bring prosperity, safety from enemies physical and spiritual, healing from disease, safety in childbirth and a good death comforted by the sacraments. Saint Sebastian, for example, was believed to protect against the plague while Saint Christopher kept travellers from harm. Saint Anthony, whose emblem was the Tau cross (pl.17), was thought to protect against ergotism or 'Saint Anthony's fire', a painful form of poisoning caused by eating rye infected with the ergot fungus. Saint Margaret, who sprang unharmed from the belly of a dragon, was sought to strengthen women in labour, and Saints Barbara and Katherine to guard against sudden death during childbirth, a common occurrence during the Middle Ages. Girdles or prayers written on rolls of parchment worn around the abdomen were believed to protect women while pregnant and in labour, and a number of rings survive that are shaped as buckled belts or girdles (pl.19). Thought to be pilgrims' souvenirs, these rings may relate to shrines of the Virgin Mary whose girdle was venerated at Padua and Le Puy.

Daily prayers and the reading of breviaries, primers and Books of Hours framed the day for individuals who keenly sought protection against the trials and dangers of daily life, and the machinations of spiritual enemies. One common belief held that virtue could be acquired by touching rings to a relic or shrine. The fifteenth-century Dominican friar Felix Faber took a bag of rings and beads belonging to friends to the Holy Land, intending to touch every shrine and relic he encountered with them so that 'they may perchance derive some sanctity from the touch'.[5] Belief in the power of rings existed at the highest level of society. In 1482 the episcopal ring of Saint Zenobius was sent from Florence to the ailing King Louis XI of France (1423–83) to cure his persistent headaches and a skin disorder feared to be leprosy.[6]

14

Gold ring engraved with the Trinity and two saints. England, 1400–1500. Inside of hoop inscribed 'En bon an' ('A good year').
V&A: M.241-1962

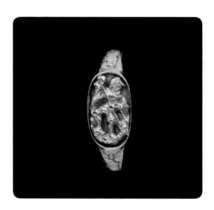

15

Gold ring with a relief of St George and the dragon. England, 1350–1400. Shoulders inscribed 'Nul si bien' ('None so fine').
V&A: M.235-1962

16

Gold ring. England, 1400–1500. Bezel engraved with St Barbara and St Christopher; hoop inscribed 'A ma vie' ('For my life'). The 13 bosses around the hoop may have been used to count out prayers, as with a rosary.
V&A: 690–1871

17

Silver ring engraved with a Tau cross.
Germany, 1500–1600.
V&A: 779–1871

18

Gold ring inscribed 'God be my help at nede'.
England, 1400–1500.
V&A: M.66–1960

19

Bronze ring inscribed 'Mater Dei memento [mei]' ('Mother of God, remember [me]').
Europe, 1400–1500.
V&A: M.225–1962

20

21

22

Contemporaries believed that a ring's power could be magnified by inscribing protective words and phrases upon the hoop. The Three Kings, whose relics are housed in a shrine in Cologne Cathedral, were believed to protect the wearer against epilepsy or the 'falling sickness' (pl.21). As the inscription on a fourteenth-century brass vessel explains, 'Caspar bore myrrh, Melchior frankincense, Balthazar gold. He who bears with him the name of the Three Kings is freed, through the Lord, from the falling sickness.'[7] Invocations combining both orthodox religion and magical words were common inscriptions on rings. The power attributed to them is explained in this invocation from a Book of Hours of 1536:

> Omnipotens + Dominus + Christus + Messias + Sother + Emanuel + Sabaoth + Adonay + ... Clemens + Caput + Otheotocos + Tetragrammaton + May these names protect and defend me from all disaster and from infirmity of body and soul, may they wholly set me free and come to my help ... May they assist me in all my necessities and defend and liberate me from all dangers, temptations and difficulties of body and soul, and from every evil, past, present and future, keep me now and in eternity.[8]

20 | Gold ring set with a wolf's tooth. England or France, 1200–1300. A later inscription inside the hoop (c.1400) reads 'Buro + Berto + Berneto + Consumatum est', a magical inscription against toothache and storms. V&A: 816-1902

21 | Gold ring. England, 1400–1500. Inscribed with the names of the Three Kings: 'Caspar, Melchior and Baltazar'. V&A: M.91-1960

22 | Gold ring. Italy, 1300–50. Bezel engraved with a merchant's mark and the name Galgano d'Chicho; hoop inscribed 'Iesus autem transiens per medium illorum ibat' ('But Jesus passing through the midst of them went His way', Luke IV.30), a verse thought to protect travellers from robbers and often found on purses and ring brooches. V&A: 88-1899

23 | Horn ring with a silver band set with a toadstone. England, 1500–1700. V&A: 711-1871

On a ring set with a wolf's tooth, the magical words 'Buro, berto, berneto' were inscribed as a charm against toothache, increasing the prophylactic power of the wolf's tooth (pl.20). The same ring bears the inscription 'Consumatum est' ('It is finished'), the last words spoken by Jesus on the Cross, which was thought to calm storms at sea and protect the voyager.

Due to its amuletic properties, toadstone was valued as highly as gemstones, despite its drab appearance (pl.23). So called because it was believed to emanate from a toad's head, toadstone is, in fact, the fossilized tooth of a prehistoric fish. In 1582 Stephen Batman described it as efficacious against the bite of spiders and 'creeping worms' and valuable because 'in presence of venimme [venom], the stone warmeth and burneth his finger that toucheth him'.[9]

23

26

Gold ring set with a Greek sapphire intaglio of
a veiled woman (c.100 BCE). England or France,
c.1300. Inscribed 'Tecta lege, lecta tege' ('Read
what has been written, hide what has been
read'), a phrase often found on seals of
this period. V&A: 89–1899

27

Gold ring set with a nicolo intaglio. Italy,
1300–50. The heraldic lion rampant on the bezel
is coupled with words spoken by Jesus on the
Cross, commonly found in prayers for the dying:
'In manus tuas Domine comendo spiritum meum'
('Into your hands, O Lord, I commend
my spirit'). V&A: M.190–1975

Rings also served official purposes: signet rings, featuring either
engraved bezels or bezels set with carved intaglios, were pressed
into warm sealing wax to authenticate documents. Coats of arms,
initials, personal devices or merchants' marks, stamped upon
bales to identify their goods, could all be employed, and wax seals
imprinted by signet rings survive on many documents, testifying to
their widespread use.

The tradition of mounting engraved intaglios in jewellery continued through the Middle Ages with ancient or Byzantine gemstones
featuring classical motifs often incorporated into rings (pl.26).
High-quality ancient gems, possibly from Rome or Venice, were
traded across Europe and sometimes set in church metalwork or
used as personal seals. A fourteenth-century Italian ring owned by
Thomas de Rogeriis de Suessa is set with a Roman intaglio of two
clasped hands (pl.28). The subject of the classical gemstone was
sometimes appropriated to serve new purposes; wearers may have
interpreted a Roman emperor as a saint, or a Hellenistic princess
as the Virgin Mary. However, individuals versed in classical
literature would have understood the original motif.

24 | Silver ring engraved with a dog.
France, 1400–1500. Inscribed 'lame
s'geein' (possibly 'J'aime songeant' or
'I love in my dreams'). Dogs symbolized
loyalty and this may have been a
personal device. V&A: 143–1907

25 | Gold ring. England, 1400–1500.
Engraved with a merchant's mark
and the initials RS. V&A: M.203–1975

Gold ring set with a Roman jasper intaglio inscribed with the initials CCPS and IPD (200–300 CE). Italy, *c.*1300–50. Bezel inscribed 'Thomas de Rogeriis de Suessa'; hoop inscribed 'Christus vincit, Christus regnat, Christus imperat' ('Christ conquers, Christ reigns, Christ rules') and 'Et verbum caro factum est et habitavit in nobis' ('And the Word was made flesh and dwelt among us', John I.14). V&A: M.275–1962

29

Silver ring. Italy, 1300–1400. Engraved with a shield and inscribed '+n notar angelis ACC' and 'Mortuus fueram arevit perieram et inventus sum' ('I was dead, I was brought to life. I was lost and I was found'). V&A: 805–1871

30

Silver ring. Probably Germany, 1400–1500. Engraved with a pair of open shears and an inscription possibly reading 'Grace'. It probably belonged to a member of a tailor's guild. V&A: M.258–1962

31

Silver ring. England, 1400–1500. Engraved with a crowned I, probably the owner's initial. V&A: 1374–1903

32

Silver ring. England, 1450–1550. Engraved with the initial W and inscribed 'God x help x williem'. V&A: M.256–1962

1500–1700

34

THE SIMPLE SHAPES of medieval rings were transformed into the triumph of the Renaissance goldsmith, as cartouches, scrolls, foliage, classical masks and colourful enamels came to adorn their new creations. Cusped bezels became the enamelled quatrefoils seen on so many portraits of the time (pl.40). Rings were set with rubies, diamonds, sapphires or emeralds, and improving or altering the colour of the gemstone by placing a tinted foil behind it became a common practice: the Italian goldsmith Benvenuto Cellini (1500–71) recorded recipes for creating different shades in his treatise on the art of jewellery. Printed ornamental drawings by artists such as Pierre Woieriot, Réné Boyvin, Daniel Mignot and Etienne Delaune show the heights of fantasy to which the goldsmith might aspire (pl.35). Goldsmiths also took inspiration from the art of ancient Greece and Rome, copying classical motifs and figures from antiquity. A delicately carved intaglio of Medusa on one ring is a fine example (pl.33).

33 | Enamelled gold ring set with a layered agate cameo of Medusa. Southern Germany, c.1580. The head of Medusa with its writhing snakes shows the quality of work achieved by Renaissance stone carvers. V&A: M.555–1910

34 | Enamelled gold ring set with a table-cut pink sapphire. Europe, c.1550. Traces of silver foil covered in a red material remain under the stone and were intended to enhance its colour. V&A: 4397–1857

35 | Designs for rings from *Le Livre de Bijouterie*, engraved by Réné Boyvin after Rosso Fiorentino or Leonard Thiry. Paris, *c.*1600. The plate shows rings in the style of the 1530s, set with cabochon and point-cut gemstones. V&A: E.397–1926

36 | Enamelled gold ring set with a ruby and diamond. Germany, *c.*1500. V&A: M.1–1959

37 | Enamelled gold ring set with a table-cut pink sapphire. Europe, *c.*1550–1600. V&A: 731–1902

36

37

Renaissance portraits and contemporary texts suggest that both men and women wore rings in profusion, from palm to fingertip, sometimes even peeping through the slashed fabric of gloves. In 1515 the Venetian ambassador described Henry VIII's hands as 'one mass of jewelled rings'.[1] While many rings were made of gold or silver, cheaper base metal alternatives were available to those with more modest purses. Children also wore rings in smaller versions of adult styles. A tiny diamond ring, which must have belonged to a very young child, was inscribed 'this spark will grow', a wish for the health and long life of its wearer (pl.38). Another small example was set with turquoise, believed to be a talisman that both protected the wearer and indicated the state of his or her health, making it an especially appropriate gemstone for a child's ring (pl.39). It was described by the poet John Donne (1572–1631) as 'a compassionate turquoise that doth tell / by looking pale the wearer is not well'.[2]

The distinction between science and magic remained hazy during this period. Belief in the theory of the humours, in which illness was caused by an imbalance between hot, cold, wet and dry humours in the body, and the sympathetic properties of inanimate objects, made possible a continuing faith in the powers of gemstones. Rings were also regarded as inherently magical. In 1546 Henry, Lord Neville, was imprisoned for commissioning a ring to guarantee success at the dice table.[3] In 1580 the courtier Sir Christopher Hatton sent a ring to Queen Elizabeth I (1533–1603) 'which hath the virtue to expel infectious airs'.[4] The unbroken circle of the ring was likewise believed to be of powerful assistance in the conjuration of demons.

38

39

38 | Gold ring for a child, set with a diamond and inscribed 'this spark will grow'. England, 1600–1700. V&A: 908–1871

39 | Enamelled gold ring for a child, set with turquoise. Europe, 1500–1600. V&A: 955–1871

40 | *A Young Woman Aged 29* by an unknown artist. Possibly southern Germany, 1582. A fashionably dressed young woman shows off her gem-set rings with enamelled quatrefoil settings. V&A: 4833–1857

ANNO. DOMINI·
· J 5 8 Z·
ÆTATIS· SVÆ. Z9·

Gemstones were selected for their significance as well as their colour and dazzle. On a sixteenth-century gold ring set with turquoise, the initials FDA and a winged heart are formed from gold openwork, suggesting that this was a love gift (pl.41). Turquoise, according to the old belief expressed in Thomas Nichol's lapidary of 1659, was 'likewise said to take away all enmity, and to reconcile man and wife', a suitable property for a romantic gift.[5] In *Li nuptiali*, written in about 1500, the Roman author Marco Antonio Altieri explained the appeal of setting both sapphires and rubies in a love ring:

> the sapphire is sky blue in colour, and denotes our soul, which derives from it; and then the balas [ruby], made of fiery matter denotes the body, receptacle of the heart, burning with amorous flame and for this reason [this type of ring] represents the gift of both the soul and the heart.[6]

Almost any gem-set, gimmel or posy ring might have served as a wedding ring in the fifteenth century, but a diamond ring was the first choice for those who could afford one. The ring's circular form, a symbol of eternity, was paired with a seemingly indestructible diamond to express the hope of an eternal, unbroken union. A manuscript in the Vatican, recording the marriage of Constanzo Sforza and Camilla D'Aragona in 1475, shows nuptial torches threaded through a diamond ring under the inscription 'Two wills, two hearts, two passions are joined in marriage by a diamond ring'.[7]

41

Gold ring set with turquoise.
Possibly Germany, 1550–1600.
V&A: M.2–1959

42

Enamelled gold ring set with a diamond.
Europe, c.1550–1600.
V&A: 730–1904

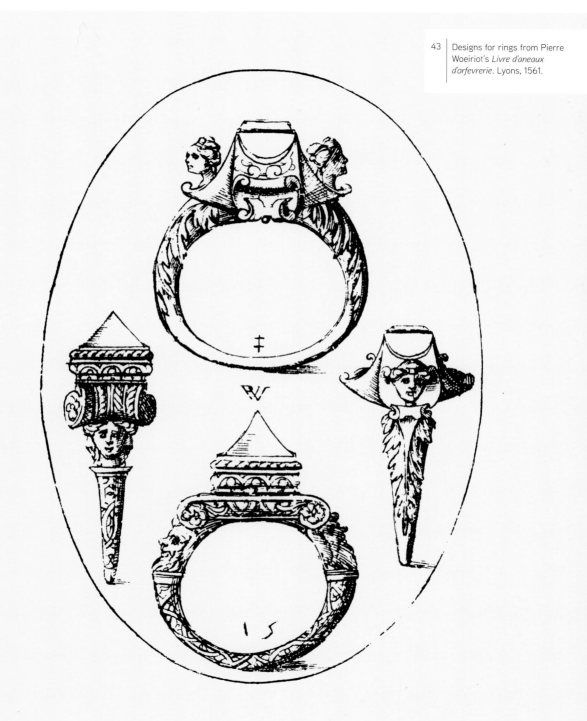

45

A description of the deathbed of Lady Catherine Grey (1540–68), the grand-daughter of Mary Tudor, illustrates how fluid contemporary views of the wedding ring were. Entrusting her jailer, Sir Owen Hopton, with her rings, she

> took out a ring with the pointed diamond and said, 'Here, Sir Owen, deliver this unto my Lord. This is the ring I received of him when I gave myself to him and gave him my faith.' When asked whether this was her wedding ring, she replied, 'No, Sir Owen, this was the ring of my assurance unto my Lord. And here is my wedding ring', taking another ring all of gold out of the same box.[8]

In this account, Lady Catherine has to distinguish between the diamond ring given to her at her betrothal and her gold wedding ring, which was presumably used in her secret wedding service in 1560. Although the prayer book of 1559 does require that a ring be exchanged in the marriage service, it does not specify which particular metal should be used. Some English Puritans condemned the use of wedding rings as 'superfluous and superstitious', but King James I (1566–1625) confessed in 1604 that he 'was married withall, and added that he thought they would prove to be scarce well married who were not married with a ring'.[9]

The fourth finger was the most usual place for the wedding ring. A longstanding belief, derived from the Roman authors Aulus Gellius and Macrobius, held that a vein ran directly from the heart to the fourth finger of the right hand so that 'rings hereon peculiarly affect the heart'.[10] By 1549, however, Edward VI's Book of Common Prayer specified the use of the left hand for weddings. In 1646, discussing the former use of the right hand, Sir Thomas Browne considered that tradition to have been based upon a 'vulgar error', or mistranslation, and that Macrobius had been speaking of the left hand all along.[11]

44 | Mirror frame in the form of a diamond ring. Painted and gilded stucco in a gilt frame, in the style of Antonio Pollaiuolo. Italy, 1470–80. The Florentine banker Cosimo di Medici used the diamond ring as an emblem, as did later members of the family.
V&A: 5887–1859

45 | Enamelled gold ring set with a point-cut diamond. Europe, 1550–1600.
V&A: 935–1871

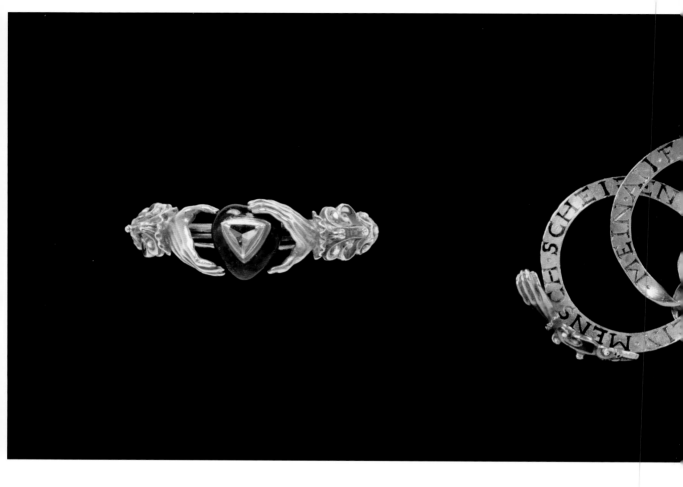

46 | Triple-hoop enamelled gold ring
set with a diamond (three views).
Germany, *c.*1600–50. Inscribed
'Mein anfanck und ende' ('My beginning
and my end') and 'Was Gott zusamen
fuget soll, kein mensch scheiden'
('What God has joined together,
let no man put asunder'), phrases
used in marriage services.
V&A: M.224–1975

47

Gold ring. England, 1600–1700.
Inscribed 'Accept this gift of honest love which
never could nor can remove' and '1. Hath tied
2. mee sure 3. whilst life 4. doth last'.
V&A: 909–1871

Gimmel rings, from the Latin *gemellus*, or twin, in which the hoop divides in two or sometimes three, were often decorated with clasped hands and hearts. Their use in weddings is suggested by the inscription of phrases used in marriage services inside the hoops (pl.46). The financier Sir Thomas Gresham (*c*.1519–79), founder of London's Royal Exchange, is said to have been married in 1544 with a gimmel ring, one hoop of which was marked 'Quod Deus conjusit' ('What God has joined together') and the other 'Homo non separet' ('Let man not set aside').[12]

Posy rings, on which a romantic verse was engraved within the hoop, were also popular for betrothals or weddings. The inscription of stock posies was a regular practice: a London jeweller asked to identify a wedding ring inscribed 'God alone made us two one', stolen in a gruesome murder in 1737, stated that 'As to the Motto of the Ring, 'tis a common one, and there may be 500 such Rings about the Town'.[13] Compendiums of posies, such as *Love's Garland, or Posies for Rings, Hand-kerchers and Gloves and such pretty tokens as Lovers send their Loves* (1674), offered lists of posies or 'epigrammes' to be placed on personal items. One young squire of 1738 entertained his lady 'with Ends of Verses, which he had got by Heart from the Academy of Compliments'.[14] This useful publication, first published in 1639, was known as *The Academy of Complements* [sic] *with Many New Additions of Songs and Catches a la mode with Variety of Complemental and Elegant Expressions of Love and Courtship*. More literate or imaginative buyers could supply their own text. The diarist Samuel Pepys (1633–1703) and his family sat composing a posy for Roger Pepys's wedding ring while waiting for their lamb to roast.

48

Gold ring. England, *c*.1600.
Inscribed 'Continnue faithfull'.
V&A: M.69–1960

49 | *Izaak Walton* by Jacob Huysmans. England, *c.*1672. Walton wears two plain gold rings on his wedding finger, having remarried shortly after his first wife's death in 1640.

50 | Enamelled gold ring with a death's head. England, 1550–1600. Bezel inscribed 'Behold the ende', its edges inscribed 'Rather death than fals fayth', while its reverse bears the initials ML, connected by a true lover's knot. This ring may have served both as a *memento mori* and a wedding ring. V&A: 13–1888

51

Enamelled gold ring set with rubies.
Europe, 1550–75.
V&A: M.280–1962

Rings could serve as reminders of the more serious matter of death. *Memento mori* ('remember you must die') rhetoric and imagery was found in poetry, paintings and on rings, and stressed the inevitability of death:

> I am but worms meat, wel I wot,
> All Fleasch is nowt but gras
> To earth and ashes out of hand
> Must all my pleasures pass.[15]

Skulls, skeletons, hourglasses and worms reminded the true Christian of the need to prepare for death and judgment. To the preacher Robert Hill, writing in 1610, it was 'the art of all arts, and the science of all sciences to learn to die'.[16] *Memento mori* rings were worn as daily reminders of death, and were sometimes set with a revolving bezel, the skull hidden behind a signet as a private message to the wearer of the truly important things in life. One such ring has a piece of bone set in the underside of the bezel, which may be a relic or simply a tangible reminder of death (pl.52). Rings engraved with skulls were referred to in Falstaff's plea: 'Do not speak like a death's head; do not bid me remember mine end.'[17]

Memento mori rings were sometimes given as memorial rings to commemorate an individual, but by the end of the seventeenth century the symbols are less frequently found. Memorial rings inscribed with the name and date of death of a friend or relative became customary, and wills specified sums to be spent on buying memorial rings for legatees. William Shakespeare's will of 1616 left 26s 8d apiece to buy rings for four of his fellow townsmen and three actors.

52

Gold ring with a piece of bone set in
the back of the bezel. England, *c*.1600.
Inscribed 'Edward Cope'.
V&A: M.273–1962

Favours distributed at funerals and weddings often included rings, gloves and ribbons. Samuel Pepys attended the burial of Captain Robert Blake at Wapping in 1661, and recorded in his diary that they 'had each of us a ring, but it [the weather] being dirty, we would not go to church with them, but with our coach we returned home'.[18] In 1685 Sir Ralph Verney reported that

> Sir Richard Piggott was buried very honourably and at a considerable charge, with two new Mourning Coaches and a [six-horse] Hearse. We that bore up the pall had Rings, Scarfs, Hat-Bands, Shamee Gloves of the best fashion … the rest of the Gentry had Rings and all the Servants Gloves.[19]

At the funeral of his five-year-old son in January 1658, John Evelyn was accompanied by 'divers of my relations and neighbours among whom I distributed rings with this motto "Dominus Abstulit" ["The Lord hath taken away"]', a quotation from the Book of Job.[20]

As well as performing symbolic roles, rings of this period continued to serve practical purposes. Signets remained an essential part of daily business, many made of plain metal with a coat of arms, entwined initials or an appropriate symbol. In an age before widespread literacy, personal marks were an important part of everyday life. Marks similar to those used by merchants to identify their goods have been found on sailors' belongings in the wreck of the Mary Rose, the flagship of Henry VIII (1491–1547), which sank in 1545.

53

Enamelled memorial ring (five views). England, 1661. Inscribed 'Samuell Nicholets obyt 17 July 1661. Christ is my portion'. Hoop pierced to reveal a band of hair and decorated with skulls, cross bones and the arms of the Nicholets family. V&A: M.156–1962

54   Gold ring with a revolving bezel
(two views). England, *c.*1600. Bezel
enamelled with a death's head and,
on its reverse, a merchant's mark,
mingling earthly and spiritual concerns.
Bezel edge inscribed 'Nosse te ipsum'
('Know yourself'). V&A: M.18–1929

55

Coats of arms were carved into translucent crystal or hardstone, placed over painted foil and set in rings worn by people of high status. Henry VIII is known to have given rings carved with his portrait to courtiers and loyal subjects (pl.58). In most surviving examples damp has corroded the bright colours of the foils, but portraits such as that of Sir Nicholas Bacon (1510–79), a courtier during the reign of Queen Elizabeth I, illustrate their original appearance (pl.56). He is shown holding a staff of office and wearing a signet ring with a brightly painted coat of arms. Sir Thomas Gresham distributed a group of similar foiled crystal rings to his friends and business associates, engraved with their arms and, on the underside of the bezel, enamelled with a grasshopper derived from his crest (pl.55). The conjunction of Gresham's crest and the arms of his associates must have served to underline the bonds between them, with the gift and wearing of the ring linking donor and recipient.

55 | Gold ring (two views) set with a reverse painted and gilded chalcedony intaglio, engraved with the arms of Sir Richard Lee and inscribed 'Flame et fame'. England, c.1554–75. The back of the bezel is enamelled with a grasshopper, the device of Sir Thomas Gresham. V&A: M.249–1928

56 | *Sir Nicholas Bacon* by an unknown artist. England, 1579.

1 5 7 9
ÆTATIS ·SVÆ· 68·
MEDIOCRIA · FIRMA ·

Loyalty to the executed King Charles I (1600–49) was expressed through rings and other jewellery set with his portrait, ranging in quality from very fine jewels to plainer objects. Although some were worn during the Civil War, many were made after the restoration of the monarchy in 1660, and continued to be collected and worn by supporters of the exiled James II (1633–1701) and his family in the eighteenth century. A fine emerald ring inscribed with the crowned monogram of James II was said to have been given by the king to his chaplain (pl.63).

Serjeants at law, the most senior members of the judiciary beneath judges, were required to present rings to the monarch and officers of the courts upon their appointment. The first recorded mention of this custom was in 1368, when Thomas Morice 'gave gold in the Lord King's Court'.[21] These rings were customarily made of plain gold and engraved with a fitting legal or patriotic motto. The custom ceased in 1875 when judges were no longer required to have served as serjeants.

58

Gold ring set with a chalcedony intaglio engraved with a portrait of Henry VIII. London, 1545–75. An impression of the intaglio survives on a document sealed by Dorothy Abington, wife of the Queen's cofferer, in 1576. V&A: M.5–1960

59

Enamelled gold memorial ring for Charles II and
Catherine of Braganza, with woven hair and gold
wire set under rock crystal. England, 1685–1705.
Charles II died in 1685 but the ring may have
been made after his wife Catherine's death
in 1705. V&A: 927–1871

60

Enamelled gold memorial ring. England, c.1649.
Revolving bezel inscribed 'Gloria' and 'Vanitas'
with the initials CR, and, on its reverse, set with
an intaglio portrait of Charles I. Hoop inscribed
'IA: the 30/1648' and 'Emigravit Gloria Angl'
('The glory of England has departed').
V&A: M.274–1962

61

Gold serjeant's ring. England, c.1525–50.
Inscribed 'Vivat rex et lex' ('Long live the King
and the Law'). V&A: M.51–1960

62

Gold serjeant's ring. England, 1576–7.
Inscribed 'Lex Regis praesidium' ('Law is the
King's protection'), a motto used at the general
call for serjeants at law in 1577. V&A: M.53–1960

63 | Gold ring set with emerald and table-cut diamonds. England, 1685–1701. The back of the bezel is engraved with the monogram of James II. V&A: M.10–1970

64 | *Alathea, Countess of Arundel and Surrey* (detail) by Daniel Mytens. The Countess is shown wearing a ring tied to her wrist by a black thread, a both fashionable and practical custom. England, *c.*1618.

The fantastical forms of Renaissance rings were gradually simplified as the seventeenth century progressed. Heavy sculptural shoulders and bezels became plainer frameworks for more abundant gemstones in the new rose cuts. In 1661 the Parisian jeweller Robert de Berquen lamented that wealthy ladies, jealous of their rivals' sparkling rose cuts, were reducing the value of their diamonds by having them re-cut.[22] Rock crystal, known in England as Bristol or Bristowe stone, was sometimes used as a substitute for diamonds (pl.67). Enamel was mostly constrained to the underside of rings, often in naturalistic floral styles (pl.65). Designs based on the botanical world by French artists such as François Lefèbre, Etienne Canteron, Gilles Legaré and Jean Toutin were disseminated through design books, creating an international style.

Rings continued to be worn in some number, sometimes tied to the wrist with a black thread, a fashion seen in contemporary portraits such as that of Alathea, Countess of Arundel and Surrey (pl.64). They could also be tied to the cuffs or hung around the neck. Writing to his wife in 1653, Henry Oxinden remarked that 'My brother had 2 rings more than I saw before upon each cuffe string, of the value of 50l the piece, besides other rings upon his fingers'.[23]

65   Enamelled gold ring (three views; facing page and below) set with pearls and an almandine garnet engraved with clasped hands. Italy, c.1640–60. V&A: 857-1871

66   Enamelled gold ring set with green glass. Europe, 1650–1700. V&A: 194-1864

67   Gold ring set with rock crystal. Europe, 1600–50. V&A: M.20-1929

65

66

67

1700–1820

IN THE EIGHTEENTH century the diamond ring became an essential accessory for the well-dressed gentleman, its importance recently illuminated by Marcia Pointon's new research. Sparkling on a manicured hand, it might dazzle buyers at James Christie's auction house, or in 1742 allow a confidence trickster to pass himself off as a baronet by appearing 'in black Velvet, with a good Watch in his Pocket, and a Diamond Ring on his Finger'.[1] The diamond ring appears frequently in contemporary portraits, including in one of Johann Christian Bach (1735–82) in which the elegantly dressed composer holds a sheet of music and wears a ring, probably set with a diamond, on his little finger (pl.68). A writer in the *Universal Spectator* lamented in 1734 that neither Demosthenes, Cicero or Quintilian had said anything about a diamond ring – 'the most necessary Qualification, in my Opinion, for a polite Orator' – and went on to explain that

> tho' the thing itself is necessary, yet the Art of using it is much more so, the displaying of a fine Brilliant glittering on the little Finger, when the hand waves gently along with a soft smooth sentence, adds an irresistible Force to whatever you deliver, gives it the Stamp of Sterling Wit, and makes it pass current.

If getting the worse of an argument, he continued,

> there is no more necessary, but to make an Extension of that Hand on which you wear your Diamond and you'll infallibly dazzle [your adversary's] Understanding, confute his Syllogism, and confound his Logic.[2]

Delicate *giardinetti*, or 'little garden', rings are some of the prettiest creations of the mid-eighteenth century. Drawing on the fashion for flowers in jewellery, silks and interior design, gemstones and glass were set in a framework of metal to create bunches and vases of flowers. A 1765 advert in the *New York Mercury* appealed for the return of 'one [ring] set in the Form of a Flower-pot, the middle a Diamond, two Sparks, three Rubies above, and an Emerald and a Topaz on each side'.[3] A charming love gift from this period was made in the form of a gold ring with an enamelled heart framing a tulip, symbolizing perfect love, inscribed 'Doux et sincere' ('Gentle and sincere') (pl.72). Rubies and diamonds were a popular combination for romantic rings, symbolizing as they did passion and eternity (pl.71).

68 | *Johann Christian Bach* by Thomas Gainsborough. England, *c.*1776.

69

Gold ring set with a table-cut yellow diamond, brilliant-cut white diamonds, rubies and emeralds in the form of a pomegranate. Europe, 1730–60. V&A: 8548-1863

70

Gold ring set with rose-cut diamonds, rubies and emeralds. Europe, 1730–60. Small, inexpensive cuts of gemstones combine to form a graceful basket of flowers. V&A: 970–1871

71

Gold and silver ring set with rubies and diamonds. Europe, c.1780. Setting the diamonds in silver enhances the whiteness of the stones; the rubies are set in gold. V&A: M.171-2007

72

Enamelled gold ring set with garnets. Possibly England, 1730–60. Inscribed 'Doux et sincere' ('Gentle and sincere'). V&A: M.170-1962

73 | Designs for *giardinetti* rings from J.B. Pouget's *Traité des pierres precieuses*. France, 1762.

74

Enamelled gold wedding ring set with rose-cut diamonds. England, c.1706. Inside of hoop inscribed 'Dudley & Katherine united 26 Mar. 1706'. V&A: 302–1867

The delicate hoops and bezels of these dainty rings presented a challenge to the maker. In 1761 the London jeweller John Leigh explained the difficulties in making

> fancy-rings, which require but a very slight shank to go about the finger, and if the ring is not made hard, the workman gets no credit by his work; for was it made of standard gold, it would bend like a bit of lead upon your finger; this is the reason we make them of a lower standard than other gold rings; let any man contradict me who can.[4]

Hearts and clasped hands continued to be used in love rings. Irish 'claddagh' rings, the name taken from a Galway village, feature hands holding a crowned heart (pl.75). The design was inspired by medieval 'fede' rings and is still commonly worn in Ireland today. The term 'claddagh' probably originated in the nineteenth century, along with a rich folklore about its origins.[5]

Rings in the rococo style, fashionable from 1730–60, were characterized by swirling, asymmetric curves and naturalistic ornament. By 1770 neoclassicism had come into fashion and rings with symmetrical oval or rectangular bezels, decorated with classical motifs or geometric patterns, were increasingly common. In 1790 a London pawnbroker described his stock as 'two old fashioned rings; the one in the form of two hearts; the other was intermixed with coloured stones, in the form of a basket of flowers'. He deemed both fit only to be broken up for the value of the materials.[6]

75

Gold 'claddagh' ring. Made by Andrew Robinson, Galway, Ireland, 1750–1800. Inside of hoop inscribed 'JMM'. V&A: M.12–1961

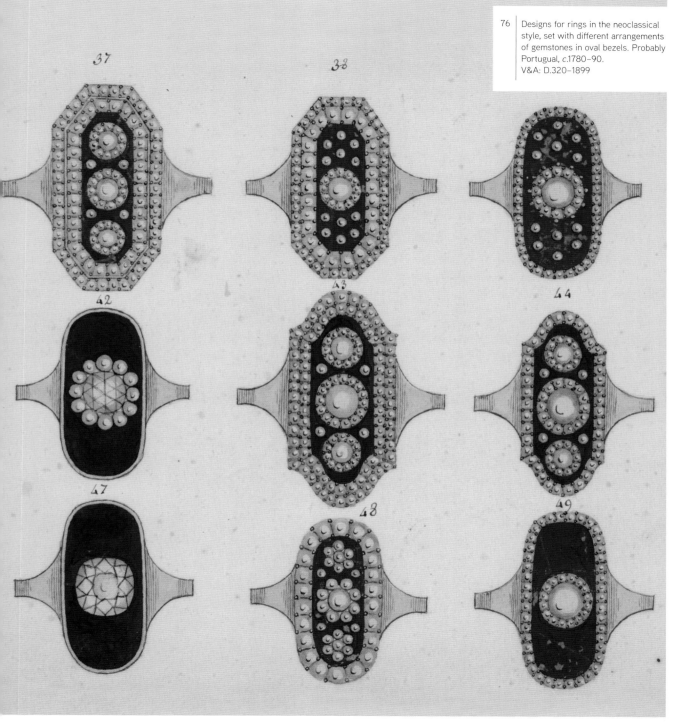

37   38

42   43   44

47   48   49

76 | Designs for rings in the neoclassical style, set with different arrangements of gemstones in oval bezels. Probably Portugual, c.1780–90. V&A: D.320–1899

Although wedding rings varied greatly in style over the centuries, their importance was always recognized. The lawful basis for a marriage was simply the exchange of vows in the present tense by the two parties, and a wedding could take place anywhere at any time of day. When determining the legitimacy of a union, however, the use of a ring became a key question. In 1706, when Robert Fielding was prosecuted for his bigamous marriage to Barbara, Duchess of Cleveland, witnesses testified to having seen the 'Ceremony of the Ring'. The ring was then

> produc'd by the Proctor of Doctors Commons, with this Device engraven in it *tibi Soli*, 'for thee alone'. The Goldsmith that made the Ring, deposed he made it by Mr. Fielding's Order, and the Device was Mr. Fielding's.[7]

Scandals such as the kidnapping of heiresses for forced marriages, often taking place in the precincts of London's Fleet Prison, and the difficulty in proving whether a wedding had occurred at all, led to calls for reform. The system was regularized by Lord Hardwicke's Marriage Act of 1753, which stipulated that a wedding could only take place in an Anglican church during the hours of daylight after full publication of the banns unless a private licence was bought, an expense beyond the means of most. As enforcement of the Marriage Act increased, the emphasis gradually shifted in legal cases from the use of a ring to the evidence of church registers and witnesses.

77 An engraving by an unknown artist depicting a Gretna Green wedding, 1791. A runaway couple are shown evading English marriage restrictions by marrying in the blacksmith's workshop at Gretna Green in Scotland.

Enamelled gold memorial ring set with rose-cut diamonds. England, 1742. Inscribed 'Matthew Arnold died 10 May 1742 aged 8 months'. V&A: M.28–2006

Gem-set hoops to secure wedding rings came into fashion towards the end of the century. Jane Austen's Isabella Thorpe, probably created in the late 1790s, daydreamed of her new life as a bride with her own carriage and a 'brilliant exhibition of hoop-rings on her finger'.[8] In 1761 King George III (1738–1820) gave a diamond hoop ring to Queen Charlotte (1744–1818) that was designed to stand no higher than the wedding ring. Mrs Papenidick, assistant keeper of the wardrobe, recalled that 'on that finger the Queen never allowed herself to wear any other in addition although fashion at times almost demanded it'.[9] George III's daughter, Princess Mary (1776–1857), wore a ring set with her father's hair at her own wedding in 1816, having 'a superstitious dread of misfortune' if she omitted it.[10] Souvenir rings continued to be given to wedding guests. At the 1791 marriage of Frederick Augustus, Duke of York (1763–1827), the second son of George III, to Princess Frederica of Prussia in Berlin, guests received a enamelled ring inscribed 'Soyez heureux' ('Be happy').

The custom of having rings made to remember friends and family endured, and became hugely popular during the eighteenth and nineteenth centuries. In 1753 Dame Anna Maria Shaw left her friend Mrs Bridges 'my new ring sett with diamonds which I made in remembrance of my late dear daughter'.[11] Although black is the colour commonly associated with death, white enamel was often used on children's memorial rings, such as on that of the eight-month-old Matthew Arnold (pl.78), as well as on the rings of those who were unmarried. Both black and white enamel were used on a mourning ring that commemorates the tragic death of seven children, possibly from an epidemic such as smallpox (pl.80). Another child's memorial ring, for the two-year-old Butterfield Harrison, shows a drooping rosebud and the inscription 'nip't in the bud', symbolizing Butterfield's short life (pl.83).

79

Enamelled gold ring set with rubies, a brilliant-cut diamond and a locket containing hair. England, c.1816. Inscribed 'Cut off 1 April 1816. Hair of King George III'. V&A: M.218–1930

80

Enamelled gold mourning ring for seven children. England, 1801–2. Inscribed 'MB Agd 16, SB Agd 12, WB Agd 10, EB Agd 9, TB Agd 7, RB Agd 5, CB Agd 2', 'Died from the 16th to the 23rd Feby. 1801'. V&A: M.18–2004

Memorial rings served to acknowledge and cement social ties, as witnessed in the will of Dame Cecilia Garrard (d.1753), in which she sets out a series of gifts:

> To my careful and skilful physician Doctor Tebb and to his lady I leave to each a mourning ring as an acknowledgment for the diligent and obliging care with which he has attended me in several dangerous fits of sickness … To my late good neighbours Mr Royston and his lady I bequeath to each a mourning ring which I beg them to accept as a token of my thanks and remembrance for their civility … And to all my kind obliging friends who have been so good to enquire after me in my late sickness, I leave to each a mourning ring as a token of my esteem and acknowledgment of their friendly civility.[12]

Mourning rings could become treasured possessions and subsequently be passed on to others. In his will of 1792 George Mason gave 'to Mr John Moncure a mourning ring of three Guineas which I desire him to wear in memory of my esteem for my much lamented friend his deceased father'.[13] Dr Samuel Buxton, a minister at Salem, Massachusetts, who died in 1758, left his heirs a quart tankard filled with mourning rings.[14] Anne Houblon, Lady Palmerston, had the mourning rings she inherited made into a pair of gold cups, bequeathed to her husband in 1735 as 'the 2 lesser Chocolate Cups you would sometimes look on as a Remembraunce of Death, and also of the fondest and Faithfullest Friend you ever had'.[15] The will of the American president George Washington (1732–99) stated that his bequest of rings to his sister-in-law was not made 'for the intrinsic value but as mementoes of my esteem and regard'.[16]

The inclusion of hair from the deceased in mourning rings gave them a very personal appeal. The London jeweller Gabriel Wirgman, who died in 1791 aged 53, left instructions in his will to have a ring made 'in the most fashionable manner with some of my hair and some of Mr Garle's father's hair' (pl.81). Mr Garle was a family friend and benefactor who had died some years earlier.[17] 'Neat and plain rings' were to be presented to Wirgman's brothers and sisters.

81

Enamelled gold memorial ring set with woven hair under a rock-crystal panel. England, 1791. Inscribed 'GabL Wirgman / Died 12 Sep 1791 / Aged 53'. This ring was presented to Mr J. Garle, son of Wirgman's old friend, as a 'particular token of remembrance'. V&A: 907–1888

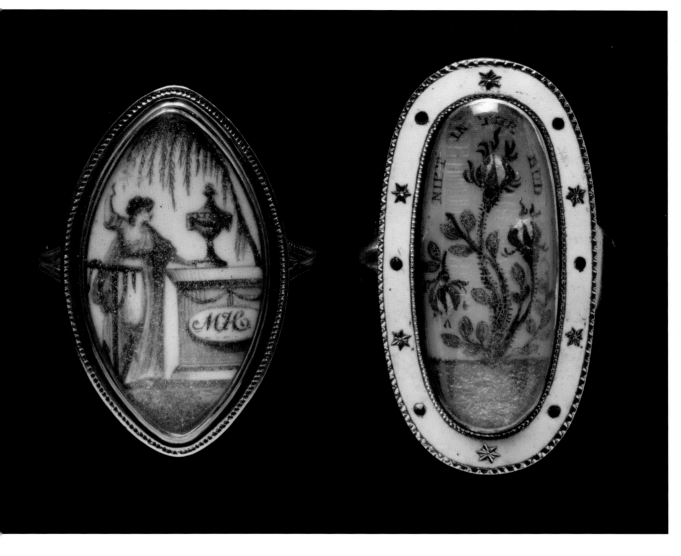

82

Gold memorial ring set with a painted sepia miniature under crystal. England, 1785. Inscribed 'Martha Holworthy ob.13 Sep 1784 aet 64'. Family records show that Martha Bolton gave birth to six children before finally marrying Daniel Holworthy in 1757. His death in 1763 led to a protracted legal quarrel with the legitimate children from his first marriage.[18]
V&A: 915–1888

83

Enamelled gold memorial ring for Butterfield Harrison, who died aged 2 years, 9 months and 14 days, with a design made of hair. England, 1792. Butterfield was the second child of Caroline and Henry Harrison, who both died within five years of his death. V&A: M.162–1962

Jewellers advertised their ability to make mourning rings neatly and expeditiously. Working in the rococo style, popular from around 1730 to 1760, they set a small gemstone or crystal in a hoop divided into scrolls, and enamelled with the name and dates of the deceased (pl.78). The London jeweller John Leigh described the work involved in making mourning rings when defending himself against an accusation of coin-clipping in 1761. He claimed that gold filings found in his possession came not from gold coins from which the edges had been dishonestly clipped, but from mourning rings made to the official 22-carat standard: 'These were filings of mourning-rings, with a great deal of scroll-work, which all jewellers know there is a great deal of filing in making one of them.'[19] The large marquise and navette bezels fashionable from 1770 offered a canvas for funeral urns, broken columns, trailing fronds, extinguished torches and grieving women bent over monuments, a visual language taken from neoclassicism.

Public figures as well as private individuals were remembered in rings. An enamelled gold memorial ring commemorates the assassination of Prime Minister Spencer Perceval (1762–1812) in the lobby of the House of Commons, which left his wife alone, pregnant with their twentieth child. It was inscribed 'Rt. Hon. Spencer Perceval died 11 May 1812 aged 49' and 'Died by the hand of an Assassin' (pl.86).

The heroic death of Admiral Nelson (1758–1805) at the Battle of Trafalgar created a great demand for memorabilia, including quantities of rings. On his deathbed Nelson himself left his hair to his lover, Emma Hamilton, most likely to be made into jewellery. Dr William Nelson, the admiral's brother, ordered mourning rings from the London jeweller John Salter for family and friends, and every admiral and post-captain who fought at Trafalgar. The death of James Newman-Newman (1767–1811), captain of HMS *Hero*, a 74-gun ship of the line, was similarly memorialized on an enamelled gold ring (pl.88). His ship sank in the Christmas Eve hurricane of 1811 off the coast of Jutland, with the loss of 600 lives.

84

One of a pair of enamelled gold mourning rings set with rose-cut diamonds, rubies, emeralds and amethysts. England, c.1787. Inscribed 'Cease thy tears, religion points on high / CS ob.25 Jan 1787 aet 70'. V&A: M.163–1962

87

One of a pair of mourning rings. England, 1792. Made five years after its counterpart possibly to commemorate a spouse or sibling. Inscribed 'IS ob.18 Sep 1792 aet 72'. V&A: M.164–1962

85

Enamelled gold memorial ring for Princess
Amelia. Made by royal jewellers Rundell, Bridge
and Rundell, London, 1810. Inscribed with the
initial A and 'Remember me'. V&A: M.151–1962

86

Enamelled gold memorial ring for Prime Minister
Spencer Perceval. Made by Samuel Glover,
London, 1812–13. V&A: M.166–1962

88

Enamelled gold memorial ring for Captain
Newman-Newman. England, c.1811. Inscribed
'Captain James Newman-Newman lost off the
Haak in the Hero 74, December 24, 1811,
aged 46'. V&A: M.314–1926

89

Enamelled gold memorial ring for Admiral
Nelson. Possibly made by John Salter, England,
c.1805. Inscribed 'Trafalgar. Lost to his country
21 October 1805, aged 47' and Nelson's motto
'Palman qui meruit feram' ('Let him who earned
it bear the palm [of victory]'). V&A: M.234–1975

90 | *The Death of Admiral, Lord Nelson*
by James Gillray,
published December 1805.

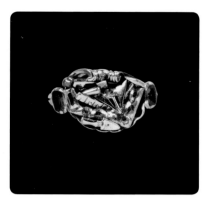

91

Gold freemason's ring set with emeralds and
rose-cut diamonds. Possibly Poland or Germany,
1750–75. V&A: 212-1870

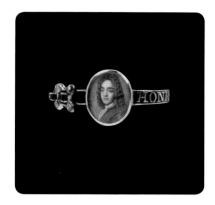

92

Enamelled and gold garter ring set with
diamonds and a portrait miniature under rock
crystal. England, c.1730–70. Inscribed with
the Knights of the Order of the Garter motto:
'Honi soit qui mal y pense' ('Shame on him
who evil thinks'). V&A: M.19–2004

93

Gold serjeant's ring. Made by Edmund Prince,
England, 1770. Inscribed 'Secundis dubiisq.
rectus', based on the Roman poet Horace:
'You possess a mind both sagacious in the
management of affairs and steady at once
in prosperous times'. This ring was given at
the general call for the serjeants at law of
Sir William Blackstone. V&A: M.58–1960

The Prince Regent, brother of Princess Amelia (1783–1810),
commissioned a group of 52 rings to commemorate his sister's
untimely death (pl.85). The youngest child of George III and
Queen Charlotte, Amelia died at the age of 27 after a long illness.
Her death caused great pain to her parents: the Princess's nurse
reported that 'the scenes of distress and crying every day ... were
melancholy beyond description'.[20]

Wearing a ring could advertise political loyalties, membership of a
club or social group, or act as a symbol of office. A late eighteenth-
century freemason's ring, probably a private commission for
a wealthy freemason, is decorated with the Masonic emblems of a
set square, ruler and compasses (pl.91). A small number of rings in
the form of a garter and with the motto of the Order of the Garter,
England's oldest chivalric order, have been found (pl.92). They
were perhaps worn by members of the Order or left as bequests.

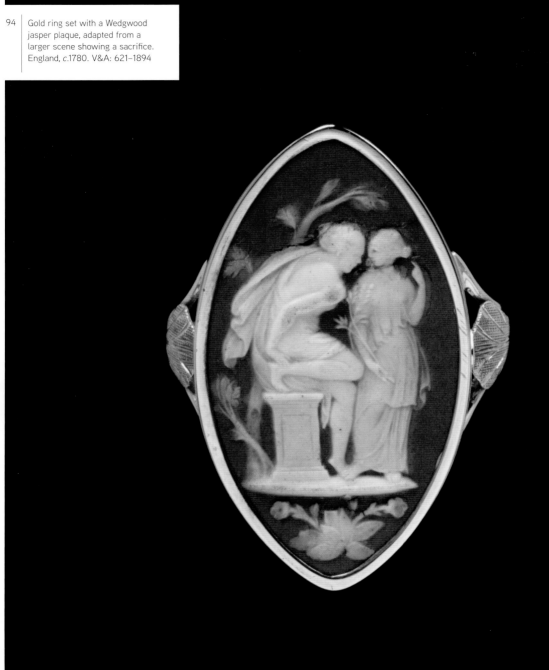

94　Gold ring set with a Wedgwood jasper plaque, adapted from a larger scene showing a sacrifice. England, c.1780. V&A: 621–1894

Stamped silver ring. France, c.1793.
Such rings were popular souvenirs
of the French Revolution in 1789.
V&A: 931–1871

Although wearing fine jewellery became unacceptable during the French Revolution of 1789, plain base-metal rings commemorating Revolutionary heroes were permitted. A silver ring from the 1790s (pl.95) bears the portraits of two heroes of the French Revolution: Jean-Paul Marat, murdered in his bath on 13 July 1791 by Charlotte Corday; and Louis-Michel Lepelletier de St Fargeau, killed on 20 January 1793 by a Royalist incensed that he had voted to behead Louis XVI (1754–93).

In 1763 James Tassie of Glasgow developed a hard glassy paste with the scientist Dr Henry Quin that was particularly suited to reproducing fine details. Tassie and his nephew William then mass-produced moulded glass portraits and imitations of ancient gems to be set in rings. The firm of Wedgwood also copied classical designs, using their trademark jasperware to create small plaques to be set in jewellery (pl.94).

96

Gold ring set with a watercolour
silhouette painted on ivory by
John Miers. England, c.1810.
V&A: M.92–2007

Silhouettes or 'profiles' were set in rings to be given to friends and lovers. They were a great commercial success as an alternative to painted miniatures because they could be reproduced quickly and cheaply. John Miers of the Strand (c.1758–1821), one of the principle exponents of the art (pl.96), advertised himself as:

> Miers (Late of Leeds) Executes profiles on Ivory to set in Rings, Lockets, Bracelets … He keeps all the original shades & can supply those he has once taken with any number of copies.[21]

Johann Kaspar Lavater's popular *Essays on Physiognomy*, published in 1775, increased the appeal of these profiles by promoting the view that a person's character could be analysed through their facial features.[22]

1820–1900

Chiselled iron ring with cast-gold figures of a muse with *putti*, possibly from models by J.B. Klagmann. Paris, *c*.1854. Made by Froment-Meurice, who died shortly before the opening of the 1855 Paris Exposition Universelle, at which the V&A bought this ring for £10.
V&A: 2658–1856

THE ROMANTIC MOVEMENT, expressed through literature, art and jewellery, rediscovered the Middle Ages and the Renaissance. Across Europe designers looked back to what were perceived as eras of superior national achievement, lost golden ages not only in politics but also in art and design. Goldsmiths drew inspiration from medieval and Renaissance models, and, in the making of jewellery, the skills of the modeller and chaser were celebrated as they had not been since the early seventeenth century. Benvenuto Cellini's autobiography, published in French in 1822, gave fresh ideas to nineteenth-century jewellers. Cellini had been the most famous Italian goldsmith of the Renaissance; in tribute, the French historicist jeweller François-Désiré Froment-Meurice (1801–55) came to be addressed as 'cher Benvenuto'.[1]

Contemporary excavations in Italy offered alternative inspiration for jewellers. The firm of Castellani in Rome was the pre-eminent exponent of neo-Etruscan gold jewellery. Eighteenth-century styles including rococo and neoclassicism were also revived, ensuring customers had no shortage of choice. From the late eighteenth century onwards, jewellery set with micro-mosaic panels, composed of minute glass tesserae (tiles), became a popular souvenir for visitors to Rome. During the 1840s micro-mosaics became less popular, until Castellani revived them (pls 102 and 103). As Alessandro Castellani would later recall:

When we took up the subject the greater number of those who followed the occupation of working in mosaic at Rome were almost unemployed … We therefore applied mosaics to classical jewellery, imitating at first the antique scenic masks, and many Greek and Latin inscriptions, and our designs were very soon copied elsewhere.[2]

98 | *Mrs Charles Augustus Howell* by Frederick Sandys. England, 1873. Mrs Howell wears a number of rings, some set with turquoise and one possibly in the shape of a serpent.

99 | Gold ring set with a cabochon sapphire. Designed by William Burges, England, *c*.1870. V&A: M.281–1975

100 | Enamelled gold ring set with a sapphire. Designed and made by Carlo Giuliano, London, *c*.1875. V&A: M.327–1922

101 | Enamelled gold ring set with brilliant-cut diamonds and a plaque by Charles Lepec featuring Psyche. Paris, *c*.1870. Bought by Harriet Bolckow, the wife of a Middlesborough steel magnate, from the jeweller Robert Phillips. Lepec was awarded a gold medal for enamelling at the 1867 Paris Exposition. V&A: 746–1890

99

100

101

Gold ring in the neoclassical style, set with a mosaic of a classical vase. Rome, *c.*1800. The angular hoop echoes the octagonal bezel.
V&A: Loan:Gilbert.164–2008

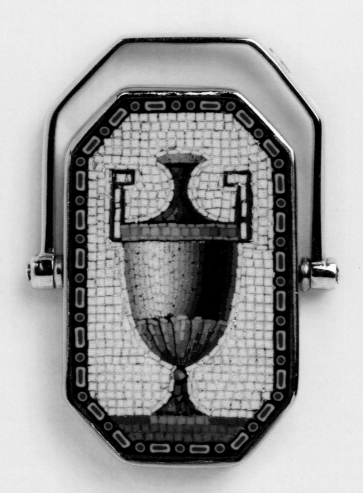

Commercial jewellery catalogues show the range of rings that were available throughout the nineteenth century. A page of rings from a catalogue by the French firm Lefebvre illustrates a number of fashionable shapes, some set with turquoises, including serpents, flowers and rings in the eighteenth-century style (pl.108). New styles emerged, including the 'cross-over' in which the hoop was split to make two ends, or was formed from two overlapping bands so that stones were set diagonally across the ring. Clusters of stones looked particularly dramatic and customers often preferred to make an impression through the glamour of the stones rather than any originality in design. An *Illustrated London News* columnist in 1887 regretted the sight of 'fine stones set in straight rows with as much notion of beauty and originality in their arrangement as in an old-fashioned box edging to a garden'.[3]

104   Gold wedding ring threaded onto a gold chain. London, 1858–9. It belonged to Jane Morris who married William Morris, artist, designer, author and visionary socialist, on 26 April 1859. V&A: M.37&A–1939

105   Gold serpent ring set with rubies, possibly once owned by George IV. England, 1800–30. V&A: 476–1903

106   Gold, glass and enamel ring. France, 1819–38. The combination of the pansies and inscription can be read as 'Pensez a votre ami' ('Think of your friend'). V&A: M.227–2007

107   Gold ring set with diamonds. England, c.1890. Inscribed with the goldsmith's mark WGM. The stones are sunk into the surface of the bezel in a gipsy setting introduced in the last quarter of the 19th century. V&A: M.23–1996

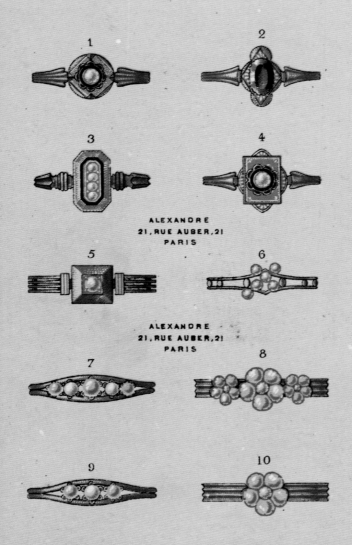

1

2

3

4

ALEXANDRE
21, RUE AUBER, 21
PARIS

5

6

ALEXANDRE
21, RUE AUBER, 21
PARIS

7

8

9

10

11

13

15

17

19

12

14

16

SOUVENIR

18

20

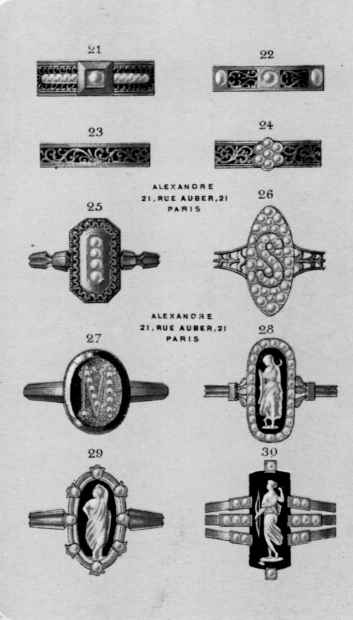

21

22

23

24

ALEXANDRE
21, RUE AUBER, 21
PARIS

25

26

ALEXANDRE
21, RUE AUBER, 21
PARIS

27

28

29

30

109

Gold ring set with a turquoise scarab and brilliant-cut diamonds. Europe or USA, 1850–1900. Archaeological excavations in the 1850s sparked a fashion for jewellery inspired by the art and mythology of ancient Egypt.
V&A: M.155–2007

Rings continued to be lovers' gifts. Motifs included flowers, hearts, acrostic jewellery using stones to spell out messages such as 'Dearest', and rebuses, in which pictures created romantic phrases. Snakes symbolized eternity, and were used on both love and mourning jewellery. An emerald-set ring in the form of a serpent was given to Queen Victoria (1819–1901) in 1839 on her engagement. Wedding rings were accorded huge symbolic value, described sentimentally by the antiquary Thomas Crofton Croker in 1853 as 'a gift far more precious than the most costly tiara of diamonds could possibly be'.[4] An act of 1855 required that all wedding rings bear hallmarks.

Gentlemen's signet rings experienced a revival in the second half of the nineteenth century, with their crest or initials preferably carved into a hardstone rather than a precious stone. One example is engraved with the arms of William Thomson, archbishop of York 1863–90, with crozier, mitre and cross (pl.111). Thomson had been a reforming head of Queen's College, Oxford, and this ring was presented to him by his Oxford friends. Excessive jewellery on men was, however, satirized: in Thackeray's eponymous novel of 1848, Major Pendennis deplored a young acquaintance, 'Did you remark the quantity of rings and jewellery he wore? That person has Scamp written on his countenance if any person had.'[5] Women, on the other hand, could wear a profusion of rings across their fingers, a fashion noted by a London footman remarking on how the elderly ladies he waited on 'dressed up monstrous fine with their jewellery'.[6]

110   Enamelled gold ring. France, 1830–60. Small hinged lids enamelled with daisies and roses open to reveal inscriptions: 'Je t'aime / un peu / beaucoup / passionnément / pas du tout' ('I love you a little / a lot / passionately / not at all'), a romantic rhyme used when plucking the petals from a daisy. V&A: M.172–1962

111   Gold ring once owned by Arch-
bishop William Thomson. Made by
Charles and William Scott, England,
1862. Engraved with Thomson's
coat of arms. V&A: M.111–1945

112

Enamelled gold ring. London, 1860–1.
Bezel inscribed 'AEI' ('Always') in diamond
sparks; inside of hoop inscribed 'Hannah Darby
died 20th Decr 1860. Aged 77'.
V&A: M.20–1970

113

Enamelled gold mourning ring in the form of
a snake, set with diamond sparks for eyes.
England, 1846. Inside of hoop inscribed
'George Edward, Earl of Waldegrave, obt.28
Sepr. 1846, aet 30'. A compartment concealed at
the back of the bezel contains plaited hair.
V&A: M.169–1962

Rings remained part of the formal apparatus of mourning. Hair was often used in designs, either incorporated in the image or dissolved into the pigment, and books of designs and instructions were available to jewellers and amateurs. *A Jeweller's Book of Patterns in Hair Work* by William Halford and Charles Young, published in about 1863, offered a great variety of designs suitable for hair jewellery; while in 1852 the *Hairworker's Manual* by William Martin addressed the fears of those who had sent treasured hair to be made into jewellery and on its return detected 'shades of other hues'. A ring in the form of a gold enamelled snake, made for the widow of George, 7th Earl Waldegrave, incorporated a locket containing his hair (pl.113). George died at the age of 30, after a disgraceful career in which he was imprisoned for drunken assault and subsequently sold the contents of the house at Strawberry Hill, which had been assembled by his distant relative Horace Walpole. Despite her husband's behaviour, his remarkable widow, Frances, became a prominent political hostess and restored the house.

114

Memorial rings gave great comfort to mourners, as Emily Palmer's description of the rings made after the death of her sister Dorothea in 1852 touchingly illustrates:

> Dear Laura [her sister-in-law] has given us each a ring of our Do's hair with a small pearl in the middle. I am so fond of it. We chose a ring – and I am glad for 3 reasons. First because always wearing it – helps me always to think of her. – 2nd because a ring seems to be a bond of love – 3rd it being round – a circle reminds one of how one's love and communion with her may and will last for ever if we don't lose it by our own fault. Then the Pearl 'Purity' pleases me so much.[7]

As with earlier Stuart jewellery, wearing a ring could advertise a person's political sympathies or show support for a cause. The French firm Froment-Meurice made rings commemorating the Prussian siege of Paris during the Franco-Prussian War, such as one inscribed in French 'United in danger, united in honour 1870–1871' and the initials AM (Ave Maria) (pl.114). They were described by *The Queen* magazine as 'some rings … which the fair Parisiennes are purchasing to present to their husbands as a souvenir of the siege and foreigners are buying as a souvenir of Paris'.[8] The wearing of rings that called for the independence of Poland–Lithuania was proscribed in 1867 under threat of severe punishment (pl.115). Poland–Lithuania had been partitioned between Russia, Prussia and the Habsburg monarchy and, after the third partition in 1795, ceased to be an independent state. Bitter struggles for independence ensued, with an unsuccessful uprising against Russian rule in 1863.

115

114 | Bronzed copper patriotic ring. Made by Froment-Meurice, France, c.1871. V&A: M.35–1982

115 | Enamelled gold and silver patriotic ring. Europe, c.1863. Engraved with the arms of Poland and Lithuania, and inscribed 'Usque ad finem' ('To the very end'). V&A: 1831–1869

116 | Enamelled gold presentation ring set with a border of brilliant-cut diamonds and the cipher of King Louis-Philippe (1773–1850). Made for the sovereign to present to an appropriate courtier. France, c.1840. V&A: M.154–1962

1900–1950

THE TWENTIETH CENTURY brought unprecedented innovation and diversity in jewellery design as developments in the fine arts were reflected in the creations of jewellers and ringmakers. The Arts and Crafts movement, begun in Britain in the last decades of the nineteenth century, took inspiration from the writings of the critic John Ruskin (1819–1900) and the designer William Morris (1835–96). Artists rejected industrial manufacturing and its effects on urban life, and looked to the Middle Ages for inspiration, aspiring to follow the working practices and design principles of medieval guilds.

Arts and Crafts designers applied principles of honest craftsmanship and 'truth to materials' to the jewellery they made. Rings made in this style show a preference for the irregularity of handwrought metals and the rounded shapes of cabochon gemstones. One of the most accomplished and innovative jewellery designers of this period was Henry Wilson (1864–1934). His 'Cathedral' ring, inspired by Gothic architecture, was designed by the architect W.R. Lethaby (1857–1931) as a wedding gift for Lethaby's wife, Edith (pls 117 and 118). Henry George Murphy (1884–1939), who had been apprenticed to Henry Wilson in 1899, became one of the finest British exponents of Arts and Crafts and Art Deco metalwork and jewellery. Their contemporary Reginald Pearson (1887–1915) was described in his obituary as a versatile artist, jeweller and engraver, whose 'hand was ever in sympathy with the material in which he worked' (pl.122).[1]

117 | Design for 'Cathedral' ring by
W.R. Lethaby. England, 1897–1901.
Lethaby annotated the design 'Dear
Wilson mine' and suggested possible
changes to the ring.
V&A: E.669:147-8–1955

118

'Cathedral' ring, gold set with amethysts, an emerald, a sapphire and a ruby. Designed by W.R. Lethaby. Made by Henry Wilson, London, 1901. V&A: M.6–1934

119

Gold ring set with a garnet. Possibly made by Carlo Giuliano, England, 1899–1903. Designed by Charles Ricketts for May Morris, the daughter of William Morris, and a talented needlewoman and jeweller. V&A: M.35–1939

120

Gold ring set with a sapphire and pearls. Designed and made by Ethel Williamson Wyatt as a gift for her mother. England, 1919. V&A: M.23–1974

121

Gold ring set with sapphires, garnets, amethysts, citrines and green tourmalines. Boston, c.1930. V&A: M.114–2007

122

Gold niello ring set with sapphires. Made by Reginald Pearson, England, c.1912. Arthur Morley Jones commissioned Pearson to produce this engagement ring for his fiancée.[2] V&A: M.31–1995

123

Gold ring set with an opal. Designed and made by A.C.C. Jahn, England, c.1901. V&A: M.79–1947

The Arts and Crafts movement was welcoming to women, many of whom studied in art colleges and studios. Amateur jewellers worked alongside professional craftsmen. Ethel Williamson Wyatt (b.1894) studied at the Manchester School of Art, where she made a ring for her mother Sophia (pl.120). She went on to work in Egypt as a teacher and in 1927 married Pat Clayton, an explorer and surveyor on whom Michael Ondaatje based the character of Peter Madox in his novel *The English Patient*. Although Arts and Crafts had its heyday in the early part of the century, some jewellers continued to work in that style up to the 1930s (pl.121).

124

The jewellers of French Art Nouveau shared the determination of the Arts and Crafts movement to create jewellery that prized artistry and design above the weight of gems and precious materials. René Lalique (1860–1945) was the pre-eminent exponent of the style in Europe. An Art Nouveau ring by A.C.C. Jahn (1865–1947), principal of the Municipal School of Art, Wolverhampton, shows the curved lines of a mermaid gazing into her opal mirror (pl.123).

125

The beginnings of Art Deco can be found in the early years of the twentieth century, but the movement came into flower at the Paris 1925 Exposition International des Arts Décoratifs et Industriels Modernes, from which the name Art Deco derives. Paris set the style for dress and jewellery in the 1920s, creating fashions copied across the world. An appetite for simplicity and symmetry was born, and some jewellers lamented what they saw as the decline of their art. In 1925 the *Jeweller and Metalworker* magazine regretted that

> The art of ring making as I knew it in days gone by seems to have disappeared. There is no elaborate carving on the shoulders now; no heavy shanks and bold settings. All that appears to be wanted is the stone, and for the purpose of setting, the least gold that can be used. This desire on the part of the wearers is a characteristic of an age which favours a plainer type of work.[3]

126

124 | Platinum ring set with brilliant-cut diamonds. Designed and made by Henry George Murphy, London, 1932. V&A: M.229–1977

125 | Watch ring set with platinum and rose- and brilliant-cut diamonds. Made by Nathan Fishberg, London, c.1925. V&A: M.241–1977

126 | Silver ring set with amethysts. Designed and made by Fred Partridge for his daughter Joan. England, c.1928. Partridge lived and worked for a time in the Arts and Crafts community in Chipping Campden and then in the Sussex village of Ditchling. V&A: M.15–1976

127 | *In the Boudoir* by Dolf van Roy. Probably Belgium, c.1916. A young woman, dressed in flowing clothes, gazes at a ring on her fourth finger, perhaps a love gift or engagement ring.

Fashionable Parisian jewellery firms such as Cartier, Mauboussin and Van Cleef & Arpels found themselves at the forefront of the new style. Large gemstones or rings set with the dense concentration of gemstones permitted by light-weight platinum settings created bold and impressive jewels. Writing in the *Goldsmiths Journal* in 1928, a contemporary noted:

> The most striking feature of the new jewellery is the large size of the stones, particularly in bracelets and rings ... In rings, large square-cut stones are the favourites, in most cases reaching all the way to the knuckle.[4]

The arts of Egypt, China and India strongly influenced Art Deco jewellers, who brought together exotic combinations of colour, such as the deep-hued coral, diamonds and black plastic of a ring by Alexandre Marchak (1892–1975; pl.130).

Arresting colour combinations were also inspired by the stage costumes that Leon Bakst created for Diaghilev's Ballets Russes, which performed in Paris from 1909; the conjunction of emeralds and sapphires became a trademark of Cartier. By 1929 diamonds and platinum were combined in predominantly white jewellery, which employed virtuoso stone cuts to great effect. Platinum became the first choice for wedding rings, often worn with a platinum and diamond solitaire engagement ring. Cartier's 'Trinity' ring, first made in 1924, with three interlocking bands of coloured gold, was an alternative romantic gift (pl.128)

Some Art Deco jewellers took inspiration from abstract art and the modernist principles of the Bauhaus school in Germany, rejecting surface ornament and exploring new materials. Designs exploited the aesthetics of the machine age and technological innovations such as the car. A group of avant-garde jewellers in Paris, including Georges Fouquet (1862–1957) and Jean Desprès (1889–1980), took innovation to the extreme (pls 129 and 131). Writing to an artist friend, Desprès explained: 'I shall focus primarily on rings. Rings are still what people like most and they're something I manage quite differently.'[5] Rings were made from base metals, less expensive gemstones and plastics.

128

128 | White, yellow and rose gold ring. France, 1940–50. The design is based on Cartier's bestselling 'Trinity' ring. V&A: M.216-2007

129 | Platinum and gold ring set with amber, jadeite and stained chalcedony. Designed and made by Georges Fouquet, Paris, *c*.1930-5. Its geometric design and choice of colours typify Art Deco principles. V&A: M.4-1980

130 | Platinum ring set with coral, diamonds and black plastic. Designed and made by Alexandre Marchak, Paris, *c*.1920-30. V&A: M.190-2007

131 | Gold and white metal ring set with diamonds. Designed and made by Jean Desprès, France, *c*.1930. V&A: M.189-2007

129

130

131

After the white jewellery of the late 1920s, the second half of the 1930s saw a return to gold, when platinum started to be requisitioned for the war effort. Ring bezels became more rounded, echoing the flowing lines of women's dresses. Baguette- and round-cut diamonds on a ring from the 1920s create a satisfying geometric design (pl.134). However, not all customers adopted the new styles. When the Prince of Wales visited Birmingham's jewellery quarter in 1931, he noted that half-hoop and cluster rings retained their popularity.[6]

The darkening political landscape and difficult economic situation of the 1930s and '40s prompted jewellers to make rings set with large, less expensive gemstones such as rock crystal, quartz and aquamarines. The designer André Arbus (1903–69) expressed the mood at the 1937 International Exhibition in Paris, stating that the aim was 'to create an atmosphere of luxury with inexpensive materials that everyone can afford, taking the resources of our time into consideration'.[7] The couturier Coco Chanel (1883–1971) echoed this sentiment, declaring that 'It is disgusting to wander round loaded with millions because one is rich: jewellery isn't meant to make you look rich, it is meant to adorn you and that is not the same thing at all'.[8] For wealthy customers, however, large gemstones were still in vogue. Hollywood stars such as Ginger Rogers (1911–95) promoted the fashion by wearing eye-catching 'rocks' (pl.132).

132 | Actress Ginger Rogers wears a ring set with a large square gemstone, 1948.

133

Gold ring set with rubies. France, *c.*1935–40.
V&A: M.209–2007

134

Platinum ring set with baguette- and
round-cut diamonds. Made by Van Cleef
& Arpels, Paris, 1920–30.
V&A: M.124–2007

135

Platinum ring set with diamonds, sapphires
and emeralds. Europe, 1920–30.
V&A: M.186–2007

136

Platinum ring set with an aquamarine,
diamonds and rubies. Made by Bailey,
Banks & Biddle Co., Philadephia, 1930–40.
V&A: M.123–2007

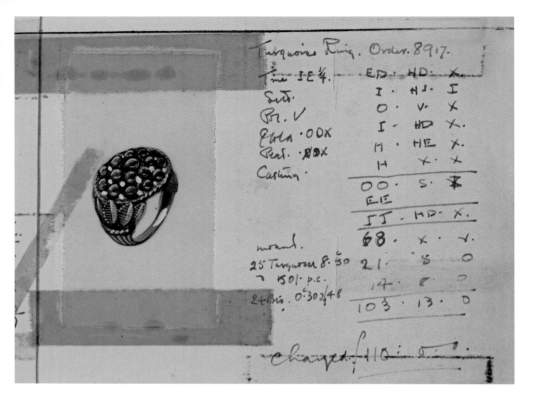

The privations of war-time took their toll on the jewellery industry in Europe. In Britain, the manufacture of jewellery was forbidden from 1 August 1942, apart from some essential items such as wedding rings. The new 'Utility' wedding rings were made of 9-carat gold rather than the traditional 22-carat and could weigh no more than two pennyweights (3.12 grams). Supply of even these rings was limited. Commentators noted that

> Public indignation, especially among service-men, is quickly rising as the scarcity of wedding rings grows more acute. The social implications of the wedding ring are obvious. Every woman in these islands who marries expects to have one, and denied the public symbol of wedlock few indeed would brave the slings and arrows of their outraged neighbours.[9]

137 | Designs for a turquoise ring for Boucheron by H. Godman, London, 1955–60. Various design possibilities are explored for this ring, especially in the arrangement of leaves forming the bezel. The design finally selected by Boucheron was pasted into the workshop ledger along with a coded costing and the final price of £110. V&A: AAD 2005/1

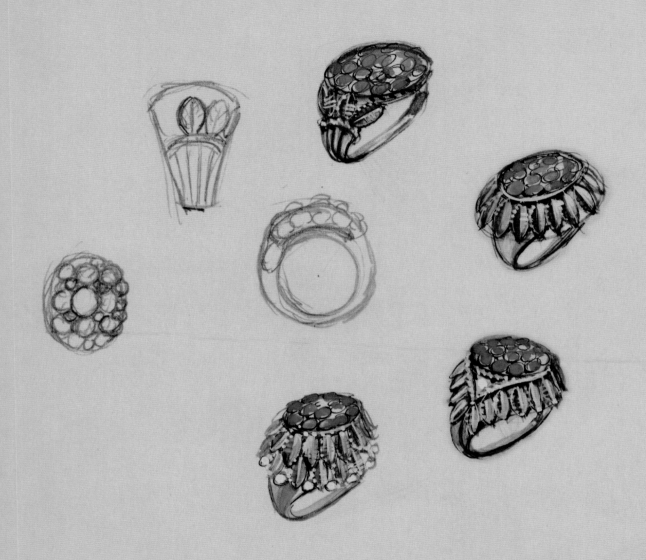

Diamonds remained fashionable for those who could afford them. Their place on wedding and engagement rings was cemented by a 1947 advertising campaign for De Beers intended to 'strengthen the tradition of the diamond engagement ring – to make it a psychological necessity'.[10] Under the slogan 'a diamond is forever', it became an enduring symbol of commitment.

Restrictions on the supply of gold continued in Britain after the war ended in 1945 and this, combined with the punishing rates of purchase tax that peaked at 125 per cent in 1947, slowed the recovery of the jewellery industry. Some wearers, however, rose above restrictions. The poet Edith Sitwell (1887–1964) was famous for her dramatic jewellery: 'I feel undressed without my rings', she told an interviewer for *The Observer* in 1959.[11] A portrait by Cecil Beaton (1904–80) shows her wearing a group of large rings probably bought from the London jeweller Michael Gosschalk (pls 138–41).

The post-war optimism of the 1950s gradually spread to the jewellery industry as clients returned to the major jewellery houses of Europe and America. The ledgers of the Bond Street firm of H. Godman (later Godman and Rabey) show the range of styles available to customers in London (pls 3 and 137). Clients of Chaumet, Boucheron and Asprey chose from a selection of designs supplied by H. Godman to the jewellery houses, and when the final version had been selected, a record with the confirmed drawing was pasted into the firm's ledger.

138 | Edith Sitwell by Cecil Beaton. She wears her customary rings, some of which are now on loan to the V&A (see below). England, July 1962.

139 | Gold ring set with a cabochon amethyst. England, c.1950. V&A: Loan:Met Anon.3–1982

140 | Gold ring set with a table-cut aquamarine. Made by Michael Gosschalk, London, c.1950. V&A: Loan:Met Anon.2–1982

141 | White gold ring set with a table-cut aquamarine and calibré-cut rubies. Made by Michael Gosschalk, London, c.1950. V&A: Loan:Met Anon.1–1982

139

140

141

1950–Present

THE 1950S AND '60s in Europe saw a desire to break with tradition in architecture, sculpture, painting and jewellery. The first jewellery courses were set up in art colleges, and rings became sculptural objects or 'wearable art'. Artist-jewellers challenged conventions about the place of jewellery in society and explored the possibilities of unusual materials.

Jewellers working independently in their studios developed their own styles, outside of mainstream fashion. As a writer in the *Daily Telegraph* explained in 1967, 'The great divide between modern and traditional jewellery becomes more and more marked'.[1] Rings became even larger and more inventive in form. Two 'Wing' rings designed by Saara Hopea-Untracht (1925–84), made in the Ossian Hopea workshop in Finland, stretch across the knuckles to cover the whole hand (pls 142 and 143). Hopea-Untracht, who grew up in a family of goldsmiths, trained in interior design and also worked with furniture, glass and textiles. She was the first jeweller in Finland to make large rings and explained her preference for the style in a 1981 interview: 'I feel an ornament should be highly visible'.[2]

As one of the first artist-jewellers in Britain, Gerda Flöckinger (b.1927) found few galleries interested in exhibiting her early work. Between 1954 and 1964 she displayed her collection at the Institute of Contemporary Art, London, an indication of her eventual success in championing jewellery as an art form. In 1971 she became the first contemporary jeweller to have a solo exhibition at the V&A. Over several years Flöckinger gave three of her rings to the museum as Christmas presents (pl.144).

142

143

144

142 | 'Wing' ring, gold set with turquoises. Designed by Saara Hopea-Untracht, Porvoo, Finland, 1959–60. V&A: M.10–2006

143 | 'Wing' ring, gold and spectrolite. Designed by Saara Hopea-Untracht, Porvoo, Finland, 1959–60. V&A: M.9–2006

144 | Silver and gold ring set with a carved citrine, a tourmaline and an opal. Designed and made by Gerda Flöckinger, England, 1969. V&A: Circ.118–1971

145 | Jeweller Andrew Grima poses with a model wearing several of his large textured gold rings set with gemstones in unusual cuts. The style would become characteristic of Grima's jewellery. England, 1966.

Gold and diamond ring. Designed and made by Jeanne Thé, London, 1964. Thé soldered tiny irregular tiles of gold together to frame the large diamond. V&A: Loan:Kalkhof1

A sharper-edged and more extravagant visibility characterizes the rings of London's Andrew Grima (1921–2007), their large colourful stones set boldly within dramatic textured settings (pl.145). It was Grima's love of stones that first inspired him to design:

[In 1948] two dealer brothers arrived at our office with a suitcase of large Brazilian stones – aquamarines, citrines, tourmalines and rough amethysts in quantities I had never seen before. I persuaded my father-in-law to buy the entire collection and I set to work designing. This was the beginning of my career.[3]

According to the *Daily Telegraph* in 1967, 'rings are probably the first item a tradition-minded woman will experiment with'.[4] On a ring designed by Jeanne Thé (1941–96), which won third prize in the De Beers Engagement Ring contest of 1964, tiny tiles of gold – each individually made and soldered together – extend right around the shank (pl.146). Experimentation extended even to the traditional circular form of the ring, with the announcement that 'a quarter of the prize-winning designs in the 1968 De Beers Diamond Engagement Ring contest are square'.[5]

Gold ring set with diamonds. Designed and made by Gillian Packard, London, 1972. Though innovative in form, the ring remains comfortable to wear. V&A: M.24–1985

Throughout the 1960s and '70s Gillian Packard (1938–97) designed rings described as 'deft, attractive and wearable'.[6] Her square ring set with diamonds can be worn in either direction and is an inventive response to the traditional diamond ring (pl.147). Artistically and commercially successful, Packard employed six assistants in her workshop on Covent Garden's Neal Street in 1966,[7] and was the first woman to become a member of the Worshipful Company of Goldsmiths in a professional capacity, rather than through inheritance.

148   Gold 'Agincourt' ring set with rubies and tourmalines. Designed by Elizabeth Gage. Made by Tom Loughridge, London, 1979. An early version of this ring won the De Beers Diamond Award in 1972 and was described as 'an engineering masterpiece'. V&A: M.21:1-2-2010

The 1970s saw the re-establishment of historicism with powerful and informed interpretations of earlier styles by Elizabeth Gage. Her innovative 'Agincourt' design, where a flexible band of gem-set panels is held by gold chains above and below, dates back to 1967 and is still in production today (pl.148).

In the 1970s precious metals were combined with acrylic, an unprecedented and daring move. Fritz Maierhofer (b.1941) had served a traditional apprenticeship in Vienna and worked for a time under Andrew Grima before he began to experiment with this new, colourful and cheap material. Drawing ideas from the London streets around him, these pieces were influenced by the vibrant colours of Pop Art and the neon hoardings of Piccadilly. The standard of craftsmanship, regardless of the value of the materials, bears witness to his rigorous training (pl.149).

Wendy Ramshaw (b.1939) won the Council of Industrial Design Award in 1972 with designs based on geometric forms, and inspired by urban architecture and the space age. She developed the idea of a 'ring set' that allows the wearer to choose the arrangement and orientation of the rings; when not worn, they are displayed on their own turned acrylic stand (pls 150 and 151).

149 | Silver and acrylic ring. Designed and made by Fritz Maierhofer, Austria, 1973. V&A: M.74–1988

150 | Enamelled gold rings, set with garnets and carnelians, sit on a turned acrylic stand. Designed and made by Wendy Ramshaw, London, 1971. V&A: M.34&A-C–1982

151 | Designs for rings and a ring set by Wendy Ramshaw. England, 1977. V&A: E.1174–1978

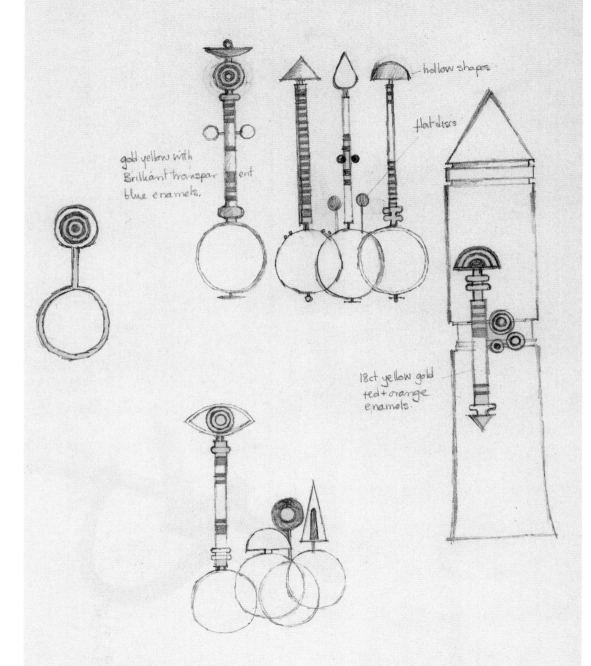

gold yellow with
Brilliant transparent
blue enamels.

hollow shapes

flat discs

18ct yellow gold
red + orange
enamels.

Artist-jewellers designed rings that were a free expression of their art. Abstract, geometric, figurative and narrative languages were all used. The rings of Kevin Coates (b.1950) unite technical brilliance with poetic inspiration drawn from mythology, literature and magic: in one ring Caliban, escaping from the pages of Shakespeare's *The Tempest*, gazes balefully from between his hands (pl.153). The work of the American designer Harold O'Connor is characterized by his interest in surface textures. He has a particular fondness for spectrolite, a feldspar discovered in Finland in 1938 that reveals brilliant hues when lit from an angle (pl.152).

Rings can express biographical and philosophical preoccupations, together with humour, wit and social criticism. Barbara Walter describes her rings as visual translations of puns inspired by fragments of conversation or daydreams; one playful ring designed by Walter allows the wearer to alter the arrangement of the figures at will (pl.154). On a ring designed by Charlotte de Syllas (b.1946), a diamond from the wedding ring of the client's mother, set topside down, resulted in a gem reminiscent of charms against the evil eye (pl.155). German goldsmith Gerd Rothmann (b.1941) pressed his own fingerprints, the unique mark of the individual, into wax to form the surface of a ring (pl.157).

152 | Gold, oxidized silver and spectrolite ring. Designed and made by Harold O'Connor, USA, 1989. V&A: M.31–2006

153 | 'Caliban' ring, cast gold set with carved grey moonstone and rubies. Designed and made by Kevin Coates, England, 1985. V&A: M.11–1986

152

153

154

'The Big Crime Ring (Size 13 ½)',
silver and steel. Designed and made
by Barbara Walter, USA, 1983.
V&A: M.40–1984

155

White gold ring set with rock crystal
and diamond. Designed and made by
Charlotte de Syllas, England, 1990–1.
V&A: M.17:1–2008

156

'Nose ring', partly patinated silver and gold.
Designed and made by Louis Mueller, USA, 1996.
Mueller often uses puns and visual jokes
to create humorous jewellery.
V&A: M.29–1996

157

'Mit den Fingerkuppen in Wachs modelliert'
('Modelled in Wax with Fingertips'), silver ring
impressed with fingerprints. Designed and made
by Gerd Rothmann, London, 1993–4.
V&A: M.41–2007

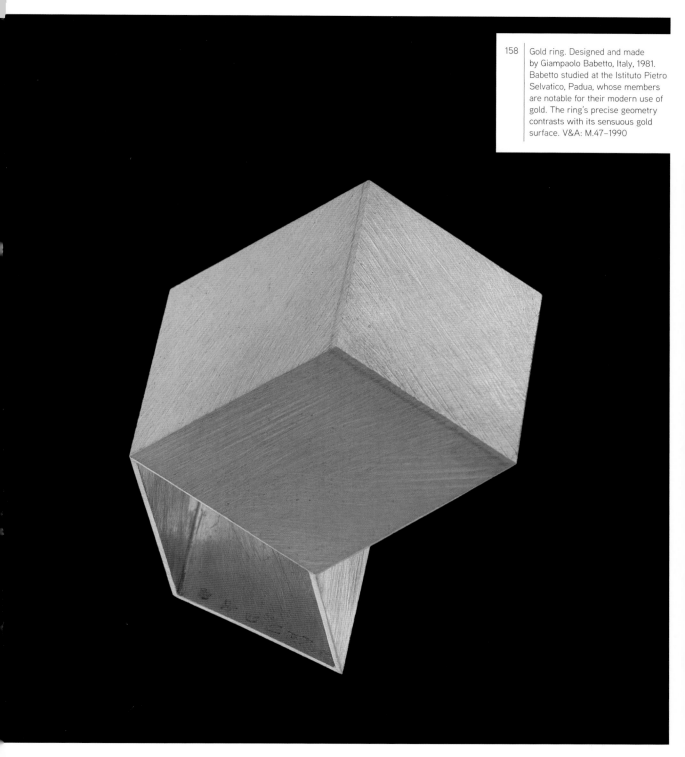

158 | Gold ring. Designed and made by Giampaolo Babetto, Italy, 1981. Babetto studied at the Istituto Pietro Selvatico, Padua, whose members are notable for their modern use of gold. The ring's precise geometry contrasts with its sensuous gold surface. V&A: M.47–1990

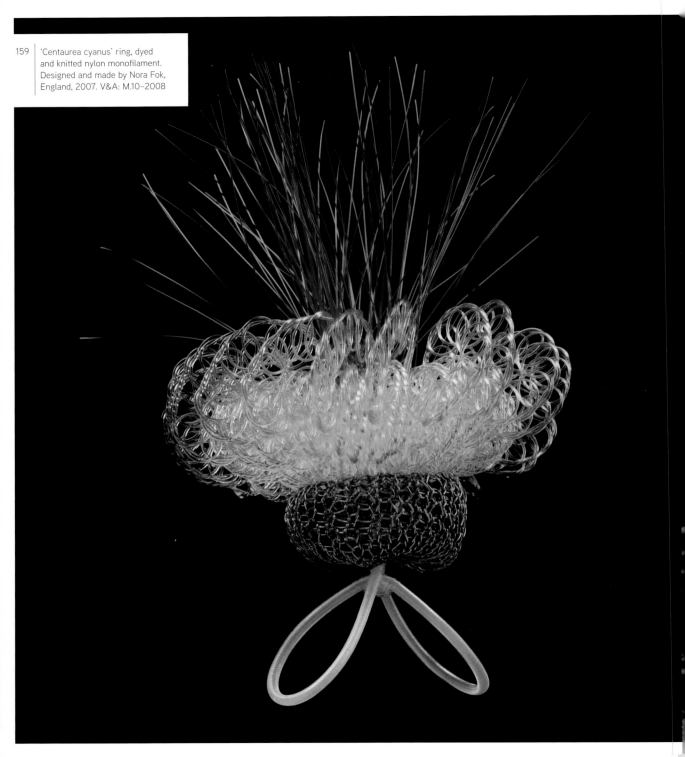

'Centaurea cyanus' ring, dyed
and knitted nylon monofilament.
Designed and made by Nora Fok,
England, 2007. V&A: M.10–2008

160

161

162

Partially gilded silver ring set with an opal triplet. Designed and made by Elisabeth Kodré Defner, London, 1990–1. Kodré Defner's jewellery unites her appreciation of nature with an interest in the properties of gemstones and crystals.
V&A: M.29–2007

Silver and gold ring set with almandine garnets and glass beads. Designed and made by Barbara Paganin, London, 2001–2. From a series based on fruit and vegetables, the ring features glass beads threaded onto gold rods that move gently with the hand. V&A: M.66–2007

Cast gold ring. Designed and made by Karl Fritsch, London, 2002–3. The gold has an almost organic quality, reflecting Fritsch's motto: 'I would like to treat gold in the same way as plasticine'. V&A: M.70–2007

Nature is an inspiration for many jewellers, including the Austrian-born Elisabeth Kodré Defner (b.1931), who during her residency at the RCA, London, transformed a leaf found in Hyde Park into a ring through lost-wax casting (pl.160). Nora Fok's (b.1952) 'Centaurea cyanus', part of the 'Nylon Botanicus' series, was inspired by a cornflower (pl.159). Jacqueline Ryan (b.1966) and Barbara Paganin (b.1961; pl.161) both begin each project with a careful examination of the natural world, and through sketches and detailed designs draw on the patterns inherent in nature to create their rings. For a gold and enamel ring made in 2007, Ryan took inspiration not from a flower but from its life-generating stamens (pl.164). As Ryan explains, it is 'the interaction of the wearer with the work which truly brings the piece to life'.

A pair of modern wedding rings by Roger Doyle (b.1947) was created by lining steel from a shotgun with gold, a technique pioneered by Malcolm Appleby (b.1946), who supplied the steel (pl.163). Peter Chang's (b.1944) training as a sculptor and his fascination with colour are apparent in his intricately constructed pieces, which often use recycled materials such as bicycle reflectors (pl.165). The irreverent jewellery of Solange Azagury-Partridge (b.1961) has been embraced by the world of celebrities and fashion. Her ring 'Hotlips' reflects the earthy, sensual side of life and exists in various colours, including a ruby-encrusted version (pls 168 and 169).

From the starting point of a hoop around the finger, contemporary jewellers have opened up a world of invention. Their rings can be playful, sculptural, glamorous or challenging, made of precious materials or the most humble everyday substances, constrained only by the imagination of their makers and wearers.

163 | Pair of wedding rings, shotgun steel lined with gold, one set with a diamond. Designed and made by Roger Doyle with steel supplied by Malcolm Appleby. England, 1997. V&A: M.7&8–2008

164

Enamelled gold ring. Designed and made
by Jacqueline Ryan, Italy, 2007.
V&A: M.47–2009

165

Acrylic and bronze ring. Designed and made
by Peter Chang, Liverpool, 2007.
V&A: M.9–2008

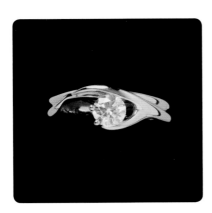

166

Gold ring set with a diamond. Designed and
made by Shaune Leane, London, 2007.
V&A: Loan:Leane.1–2007

167

'Raindance' ring, platinum set with diamonds.
Made by Boodles, England, 2009.
V&A: M.52:1–2009

168 | Publicity photograph for the jewellery
of Solange Azagury-Partridge.
Model Susie Cave wears 'Witchy',
'Hotlips' and 'Flat Fringe' rings,
and a diamond-beaded bracelet.
Photograph by Katharina Jebb.

169 | 'Hotlips' ring, silver and enamel.
Designed and made by Solange
Azagury-Partridge, England, 2007.
V&A: M.22–2008

169

NOTES

INTRODUCTION

1   Old Bailey Proceedings Online (www.oldbaileyonline.org, 24 July 2010), January 1761, trial of John Leigh (t17610116–5)
2   Julia Blackburn, *Charles Waterton, 1782–1865: Traveller and Conservationist* (London, 1989), p.162
3   'Dactyliotheca Watertoniana: A Descriptive Catalogue of the Finger-rings in the Collection of Mrs. Waterton' (manuscript), 1866, now in the National Art Library, London
4   Blackburn, p.215 (cited note 2)

1200–1500

1   Margaret Wade Labarge, *Mistress, Maids and Men: Baronial Life in the Thirteenth Century* (London, 1965, reprinted 2003), p.145
2   Ibid.
3   John Jay Parry, *The Art of Courtly Love: With Introduction, Translation and Notes* (New York, 1941), p.176
4   Diamond Trading Company, *Diamonds and the Power of Love* (London, 2002), p.16
5   A. Stewart (ed.), *The Book of the Wanderings of Felix Fabri* (Palestine Pilgrims Text Society, 1882–97), vol.I, part 1, p.93
6   Sally J. Cornelison, 'A French King and a Magic Ring: The Girolami and a Relic of St Zenobius in Renaissance Florence', *Renaissance Quarterly* (2002), vol.LV, pp.434–69
7   Joan Evans, *Magical Jewels of the Middle Ages and the Renaissance: Particularly in England* (London, 1922, reprinted 2004), p.126
8   Eamon Duffy, *The Stripping of the Altars: Traditional Religion in England 1400–1580* (London, 1992), p.274
9   Christopher J. Duffin, 'Fossils as Drugs: Pharmaceutical Palaeontology', *Ferrantia* (2008), vol.LIV, p.43

1500–1700

1   Diana Scarisbrick, *Rings: Symbols of Wealth, Power and Affection* (London, 1993), p.42
2   John Donne, *The Complete English Poems*, ed. Albert Smith (London, 1996), p.279
3   Alec Ryrie, *The Sorcerer's Tale* (Oxford, 2008)
4   Mary E. Hazard, *Elizabethan Silent Language* (Nebraska, 2000), p.115
5   Jackson Campbell Boswell, 'Shylock's Turquoise Ring', *Shakespeare Quarterly* (Autumn 1963), vol.XIV, no.4, pp.481–3
6   M. Ajmar-Wollheim and F. Dennis (eds), *At Home in Renaissance Italy* (London, 2006), p.110
7   Diamond Trading Company, pp.12–13 (cited note 4, 1200–1500)
8   William M. Schutte, 'Thomas Churchyard's "Dollful Discourse" and the Death of Lady Catherine Grey', *The Sixteenth Century Journal* (Winter 1984), vol.XV, no.4, pp.471–87

9   David Cressy, *Birth, Marriage and Death: Ritual, Religion, and the Life Cycle in Tudor and Stuart England* (Oxford, 1997), p.345
10 Sir Thomas Browne, *Pseudodoxia Epidemica* IV (1646, sixth edition 1672), iv ('Of the Ring finger')
11 Ibid.
12 John William Burgon, *The Life and Times of Sir Thomas Gresham*, vol.I (London, 1839), pp.51–2
13 Old Bailey Proceedings Online (www.oldbaileyonline.org, 24 July 2010), July 1737, trial of Hans MacConnel (t17370706-16)
14 Old Bailey Proceedings Online (www.oldbaileyonline.org, 24 July 2010), 8 November 1738, Ordinary's Account (OA17381108)
15 Schutte, pp.471–87 (cited note 8)
16 Robert Hill, *The Pathway to Prayer and Pietie*, 1610, quoted in Cressy, p.389 (cited note 9)
17 William Shakespeare, *Henry IV* Part 2, II, iv
18 Diary of Samuel Pepys, Saturday 13 April 1661 (www.pepysdiary.com, 25 July 2010)
19 *Memoirs of the Verney Family*, 1642–96, vol.IV, p.327; quoted in P. Cunington and C. Lucas, *Costume for Birth, Marriage and Death* (London, 1972), p.192
20 Clare Gittings, *Death, Burial and the Individual in Early Modern England* (London, 1988), p.81
21 J.H. Baker (Selden Society), *The Order of Serjeants at Law* (London, 1984), p.94, quoted in Mark Emanuel, *The Surviving Rings of the Serjeants at Law*, 2008, private publication (copy held in the Metalwork Department library, Victoria and Albert Museum)
22 Robert de Berquen, *Merveilles des Indes Occidentales et Orientales*, 1661, quoted in D. Scarisbrick, C. Vachaudez and J. Walgrave (eds), *Brilliant Europe: Jewels from European Courts* (Brussels, 2007), p.125
23 Sir Thomas Peyton of Knowlton and their circle, *The Oxinden and Peyton Letters 1642–1670: Being the Correspondence of Henry Oxinden of Barham,* (London, 1937), p.190

1700–1820

1   Old Bailey Proceedings Online (www.oldbaileyonline.org, 24 July 2010), January 1742, Ordinary's Account (OA17420113)
2   Marcia Pointon, *Brilliant Effects: A Cultural History of Gem Stones and Jewellery* (London, 2009), p.58
3   Martha Gandy Fales, *Jewelry in America 1600-1900* (Suffolk, 1995), p.31
4   Old Bailey Proceedings Online (www.oldbaileyonline.org, 24 July 2010), January 1761, trial of John Leigh (t17610116-5)
5   Ida Delamer, 'The Claddagh Ring', *Irish Arts Review Yearbook* (1996), vol.XII, pp.181–7
6   Old Bailey Proceedings Online (www.oldbaileyonline.org, 24 July 2010), May 1790, trial of Thomas Hopkins (t17900526-1)
7   Old Bailey Proceedings Online (www.oldbaileyonline.org, 24 July 2010), December 1706, trial of Robert Fielding (t17061206-1)

8   Jane Austen, *Northanger Abbey* (1817), ch.15
9   Jane Roberts (ed.), *George III and Queen Charlotte: Patronage, Collecting and Court Taste* (London, 2004), cat.442
10 Diana Scarisbrick, *Jewellery in Britain: 1066–1837* (Norwich, 1994), p.339
11 Marcia Pointon, *Strategies for Showing: Women, Possession and Representation in English Visual Culture 1665–1800* (Oxford, 1997), p.373
12 Ibid., p.382
13 The last will and testament of George Mason, www.virginia1774.org/GeorgeMasonWill.html, 27 July 2010
14 Alice Morse Earle, *Customs and Fashions in Old New England* (Gloucestershire, 2009), p.200
15 The chocolate cups are now in the British Museum, MLA 2005,6–4.1 and 2
16 Diana Scarisbrick, *Rings: Jewelry of Power, Love and Loyalty* (London, 2007), p.179
17 Simon Bendall, 'A Group of Mourning Rings', *Jewellery Studies* (2008), vol.XI, pp.91–103
18 Email correspondence between Clare Phillips and Mary Fraser, 20 September 2009.
19 Old Bailey Proceedings Online (www.oldbaileyonline.org, 24 July 2010), January 1761, trial of John Leigh (t17610116-5)
20 Christopher Hibbert, *George III: A Personal History* (London, 1999), p.394
21 Trade label on the back of a portrait of Isabella Burrell (V&A: P.82-1929)
22 Johann Kaspar Lavater, *Physiognomische Fragmente zur Beförderung der Menschenkenntnis und Menschenliebe* (1775–8)

1820–1900

1   Simon Jervis, *Art and Design in Europe and America, 1800–1900* (London, 1987), p.80
2   Geoffrey Munn, *Castellani and Giuliano: Revivalist Jewellers of the 19th Century* (New York, 1984), p.117
3   Scarisbrick (1993), p.164 (cited note 1, 1500–1700)
4   *Catalogue of a Collection of Ancient and Medieval Rings and Personal Ornaments Formed for Lady Londesborough* (London, 1853), quoted in Tetzeli von Rosador, 'Gems and Jewellery in Victorian Fiction', *R.E.A.L.* (1984), vol.II, pp.275–318
5   William Makepeace Thackeray, *Pendennis* (1848), quoted in von Rosador (cited note 4)
6   O. Collings and G. Reddington, *Georgian Jewellery, 1714–1830* (London, 2007), p.88
7   Pat Jalland, *Death in the Victorian Family* (Oxford, 1996), pp.298–9
8   Scarisbrick (1993), p.166 (cited note 1, 1500–1700)

1900–1950

1   Obituary in *The Apple (of beauty and of discord)*, 1920, p.174
2   Pearson would later be reported missing, presumed killed, near Hooge, Belgium, on 16 June 1915
3   *Jeweller and Metalworker* (15 August 1925), p.1160
4   'The Mode in Jewellery', *Goldsmiths Journal* (September 1928), pp.826–7
5   Melissa Gabardi, *Jean Després: Jeweller, Maker and Designer of the Machine Age* (London, 2008), p.110
6   Clare Phillips, 'Art Deco Jewellery', in C. Benton, T. Benton and G. Wood (eds), *Art Deco: 1910–39* (London, 2003), p.279
7   Gilles Chazal, *The Art of Cartier* (Paris, 1989), p.93
8   Michael Batterberry, *Fashion: The Mirror of History* (London, 1982), p.319
9   Shena Mason, *Jewellery Making in Birmingham 1750–1995* (Chichester, 1998), p.137
10 Edward Jay Epstein, 'Have You Ever Tried to Sell a Diamond?', *The Atlantic Magazine* (February 1982)
11 Edith Sitwell, 'My clothes and I', *Observer* (18 May 1959), p.19

1950–PRESENT

1   Nicola Hemingway, 'Rings on All her Fingers', *Daily Telegraph* (27 March 1967), p.5
2   Oppi Untracht, *Saara Hopea-Untracht: Life and Work* (Helsinki 1988), p.190
3   Veronica Horwell, Obituary for Andrew Grima, *Guardian* (18 January 2008), p.42
4   Hemingway (cited note 1)
5   'Square Shank Rings Theme for '68?', *Retail Jeweller* (24 April 1968)
6   Peter Hinks, *Twentieth-Century British Jewellery 1900–1980* (London, 1983), p.132
7   Fiona MacCarthy, 'A Short Guide to Modern British Jewellery', *Guardian* (4 November 1966)

FURTHER READING

Bury, Shirley, *Introduction to Rings* (London, 1984)

Campbell, Marian, *Medieval Jewellery* (London, 2009)

Chadour, Beatriz, *Rings: The Alice and Louis Koch Collection* (Leeds, 1994)

Cherry, John et al., *The Ring* (London, 1981)

Dalton, O.M., *Catalogue of the Finger Rings, Early Christian, Byzantine, Teutonic, Medieval and Later in the British Museum* (London, 1912)

Henig, M. and Scarisbrick, D., *Finger Rings from Ancient to Modern* (Oxford, 2003)

Oman, Charles, *Catalogue of Rings in the Victoria and Albert Museum* (London, 1930, reprinted Ipswich, 1993)

Phillips, Clare, *Jewels and Jewellery* (London 2000, revised 2008)

Pointon, Marcia, *Brilliant Effects: A Cultural History of Gem Stones and Jewellery* (New Haven and London, 2009)

Scarisbrick, Diana, *Rings: Symbols of Wealth, Power and Affection* (London, 1993)

—, *Historic Rings: Four Thousand Years of Craftsmanship* (Tokyo, 2004)

—, *Rings: Jewellery of Power, Love and Loyalty* (London, 2007)

ACKNOWLEDGEMENTS

I owe my gratitude to many people – to Richard Edgcumbe and Beatriz Chadour-Sampson first of all, for all their help, advice and encouragement, and for reading many versions of the text with great patience. Clare Phillips provided invaluable help and advice and Veronica Bevan worked tirelessly cross-referencing images. Any remaining errors in fact or judgment are entirely my own. To Dominic Naish, Ian Thomas and Richard Davis for the wonderful photographs, and to Jo Whalley for her work in identifying the gemstones and gemmological advice. Thanks must go to Tessa Murdoch and all my colleagues in the Metalwork section for their support. Many thanks to Charlotte Heal, Laura Lappin, Laura Potter and V&A Publishing for their enthusiasm and help. And, of course, to Paul, Oscar and Miranda for putting up with it all!

PICTURE CREDITS

Certain objects have been acquired by the V&A through the generosity of the individuals or organisations listed below (in alphabetical order by institution or surname with corresponding plate numbers).

Given by the American Friends of the V&A through the generosity of Patricia V. Goldstein: 71, 96, 121, 128, 130, 131, 133, 134, 135 and 136

Given by the American and International Friends of the V&A through the generosity of Franklin and Susie Parrasch: 156

Given by Solange Azagury-Partridge: 168

Given in memory of Martin Buckmaster: 63

Bequeathed by Mrs Ann Cameron: 58

Bought with funds from L.C.G. Clarke: 55

Given by Martha Connell: 152

Given by Gil Devlin in memory of his wife Mara Amats: 163

Given by Dame Joan Evans: 4, 5, 7, 9, 10, 13, 14, 15, 18, 19, 21, 25, 27, 28, 30, 36, 41, 46, 48, 51, 52, 60, 61, 62, 72, 83, 84, 85, 86, 87, 89, 99, 110 and 113

Supported by the Friends of the V&A: 165

Given by Elizabeth Gage: 148

Given by Jacqueline and Jonathan Gestetner: 164

Given by Wendy Ramshaw: 150, 151

Royal College of Art Visiting Artists Collection: 157, 160, 161, 162

Salting Bequest: 33

Given by Gulderen Tekvar in memory of her mother: 155

Given by Oppi Untracht: 142, 143

Images and copyright clearance have been kindly supplied as listed below (in alphabetical order by institution or surname with corresponding plate numbers). All other illustrations, unless otherwise stated, are © V&A Images.

© ADAGP, Paris and DACS, London 2011: 129

Courtesy of Solange Azagury-Partridge / Photo: Katerina Jebb: 168

Courtesy of Giampaolo Babetto / Photo: Giustino Chemello, Vicenza: 158

© Bibliothèque nationale de France: 6

© Birmingham Museums & Art Gallery: 98

© Bridgeman Art Library: 1, 56, 68, 90, 127, p.12, p.28, p.56

© Corbis: p.92, 132

© Gerda Flöckinger CBE: 144

© Getty Images: 145

© Shaun Leane: 166

© Fritz Maierhofer: 149

© Marchak, Paris: 130

© Mary Evans Picture Library/Alamy: 77

© Louis Mueller: 156

© National Portrait Gallery, London: 49, 64

© Rex Features: front jacket

© Sotheby's Picture Library: 138

© Estate of Gillian Packard: 147

© Estate of Jeanne Thé: 146

© Barbara Walter: 154

INDEX

Page numbers in *italic* refer to illustration captions.